THE AMERICAN
PIT BULL TERRIER

Cynthia P. Gallagher

The American Pit Bull Terrier

Project Team
Editor: Stephanie Fornino
Copy Editor: Joann Woy
Design: Stephanie Krautheim
Series Design: Stephanie Krautheim and Mada Design
Series Originator: Dominique De Vito

T.F.H. Publications
President/CEO: Glen S. Axelrod
Executive Vice President: Mark E. Johnson
Publisher: Christopher T. Reggio
Production Manager: Kathy Bontz

T.F.H. Publications, Inc.
One TFH Plaza
Third and Union Avenues
Neptune City, NJ 07753

Printed and bound in China

07 08 09 10   3 5 7 9 8 6 4 2

ISBN 978-079383625-3
Library of Congress Cataloging-in-Publication Data
Gallagher, Cynthia P. The American pit bull terrier / Cynthia P. Gallagher.
p. cm.
Includes index.
ISBN 0-7938-3625-5 (alk. paper)
1. American pit bull terrier. I. Title.
SF429.A72G35 2006

  636.755'9--dc22

This book has been published with the intent to provide accurate and authoritative information in regard to the subject matter within. While every precaution has been taken in preparation of this book, the author and publisher expressly disclaim responsibility for any errors, omissions, or adverse effects arising from the use or application of the information contained herein. The techniques and suggestions are used at the reader's discretion and are not to be considered a substitute for veterinary care. If you suspect a medical problem consult your veterinarian.

The Leader In Responsible Animal Care For Over 50 Years!™
www.tfhpublications.com

TABLE OF CONTENTS

1

HISTORY

of the American Pit Bull Terrier

"**G**ive a dog a bad name and hang him. The virtues of the dog are his own; his vices, those of his master." —Old English Proverb

Perhaps no breed of dog ever has been given as bad a name as the American Pit Bull Terrier (APBT). The mere mention of the ambiguous term "pit bull" conjures images of a vicious and aggressive canine monster with a taste for small children. Likewise, "pit bull" owners are automatically tagged as promoters of the cruel and illegal practice of dog fighting.

Nothing could be further from the truth. In fact, the APBT was once one of the most respected and beloved breeds in the United States. Ignorance and hype have fostered its negative reputation, putting the breed in real danger of extinction. Through education and awareness, though, the public can be shown the virtues of this much-maligned dog breed.

First things first: There is no such dog as a "pit bull." This catch-all moniker is too frequently attached to any poorly bred fighting dog, regardless of his lineage. A "pit bull" may have strains of APBT, American Staffordshire Terrier, Staffordshire Bull Terrier, Bull Terrier, Boxer, or any combination thereof. No self-respecting APBT owner would refer to his dog as a "pit bull."

To really understand the nuances at stake, we need to examine the origins of the breed.

EARLY DEVELOPMENT OF THE APBT

During ancient times of Roman circuses and barbaric wars, no specific dog breed names existed as we know them today. Dogs were named for the type of work performed.

Though descended from ancient times and civilizations, the dog we know as the American Pit Bull Terrier is a comparatively recent breed. Only in the last 60 years was the APBT bred separately from the American Staffordshire Terrier (AmStaff), although they have the same origins and are very similar in appearance. Both descend from early Greek Mastiff-type dogs called Molossians who found their way into fighting arenas throughout the Roman Empire, entertaining barbaric civilizations by fighting every kind of creature, from human to elephant. Professional warriors who rode into battle side by side with these canine gladiators prized their savage fighting ability. One Egyptian pharaoh kept a retinue of 2,000 fighting dogs in his army.

During the Middle Ages, mechanical weapons and armaments began to surpass the destructive power of the Mastiffs, and the nobility began using animals as guard dogs and hunters of wolves, bears, and other large marauders. Impressed with these dogs' strength and tenacity, Europeans began matching them against other beasts as a mini-spectacle and ultimately as a full-fledged sport. Bull-and bearbaiting, which originated in Germany with the *bullenbeisser* and the *barenbeisser* dogs, became popular

APBT Myths

Myth: "Pit bulls" bite more people than any other breed.

Truth: Accurate records by breed are seldom kept, but available records show this to be false. The Dallas, Texas suburb of Farmers Branch has kept accurate records of dog bites by breed since 1980. From 1980 to 1987, out of a total 1,593 dog bites, only 30 of those were by "pit bulls." That figure may actually be even lower for true APBTs, as so many mixed breeds with similar characteristics are mistaken for APBTs and randomly termed "pit bulls."

Myth: APBTs lock their jaws to the death.

Truth: This notion is applicable to the APBT's tenacity rather than a physiological ability.

Myth: All APBTs are dangerous and should be banned.

Truth: There always seems to be a breed that is looked upon as bad or dangerous. The Doberman Pinscher has endured that stigma, and so has the Rottweiler. Regardless of the breed, any dog who is not socialized or well bred has the potential to be a threat to society. If we pass breed-specific laws against one type of dog, we ignore many other breeds that have the potential to attack humans.

throughout Europe. Crowds gathered in every village and town square to watch one or more Mastiffs attack a chained bull.

Although these great dogs had plenty of courage, they lacked agility. The bulls' horns frequently gored the dogs or tossed them up to 50 feet (15.2 m) in the air. Many died in the bullbaiting encounters, leaving only the quickest dogs to dominate the gene pools. These smaller, faster descendants became known as "Bulldogs" and gradually replaced the Mastiffs in blood sports.

The German city of Brabant became the breeding center for smaller, shorter-legged *bullenbeissers*. These well-muscled, medium-sized Brabanter dogs looked very much like early English Bulldogs, which in turn look like the APBTs of today.

THE APBT IN GREAT BRITAIN

During the sixth century B.C., Phoenician traders brought some of their Molossian dogs to England, where they flourished and became the forbears of the early English Mastiffs. These super-sized, ferocious canines fought alongside their masters against Roman invaders. Impressed with the warrior dogs, the Romans sent many of them back to Rome. There, the dogs became known as *pugnaces* (broad-mouthed) and were soon stars of the bloody Roman circuses, pitted against armed men, other animals, and each other.

As these Mastiff dogs became popular for specific activities, breeding became more selective, and breed names were created to reflect their distinctive purposes. Dogs who fought bulls or bears throughout continental Europe became known as Bulldogs, while in England, the massive dogs used for protection remained Mastiffs.

Bull- and bearbaiting events were public spectacles that drew large crowds and provided a diversion from

Today's APBT descends from early Greek Mastiff-type dogs.

the drudgery of daily life for most Britons. These barbaric activities were finally banned by the Humane Acts of 1835, which brought bull- and bearbaiting to a halt. Dog fighting unfortunately continued, albeit in secret. You couldn't very well hold a clandestine bearbait, but it was easy to pit two dogs against each other in a dark cellar or back room.

Along with cock fighting, dog fighting flourished into a widespread subculture that became a way of life. Not only did it provide "entertainment," but it put food on the table for many an out-of-work Briton and was taken very seriously by participants. Rules were officially established and logbooks maintained. People began experimenting with crossbreeding in a quest for a dog who combined the ferocity and strength of the Bulldog with the agility and tenacity of a terrier. The result was the bull-and-terrier, or *half-and-half*, smaller and better suited than Bulldogs to following small game into their underground (*terra*) dens but just as fierce and powerful in the fighting ring. They were also gentle and affectionate toward the humans with whom they lived.

Characteristics of the APBT

- Strong desire to please his owner
- Protective instinct toward family
- Enjoys being the center of attention
- Intelligent and highly trainable
- Robust and energetic
- Good with children

Toward the end of the nineteenth century, another group of bull-and-terriers branched off into a distinctive breed ultimately acknowledged by the Kennel Club (KC) in 1935: the Bull Terrier. Selective breeding in this dog produced an elongated head and an appearance quite different from the bull-and-terriers, who had become especially popular in the Staffordshire area of England. To avoid confusion with the Bull Terrier, the half-and-half was renamed the Staffordshire Bull Terrier (Staffy Bull).

The Staffy Bull is thus descended from the pit-fighting dog and is the APBT's closest English relative. Staffordshire Bull

Terriers are energetic little charmers who stand from 13 (33.0 cm) to 16 inches (40.6 cm) tall and should weigh no more than 40 pounds (18.1 kg). It is the most popular terrier breed in England today. The APBT as Americans know him does not exist in England.

THE APBT IN THE UNITED STATES

APBTs in America can be traced to the late seventeenth century, when English and Irish working-class immigrants came to the United States with their Bulldog–terrier mixes. The newcomers popularized dog fighting until it was as prevalent and widely accepted as in Europe. As in Great Britain, Americans readily embraced the sport as a release from the tedium and rigor of their daily lives and began to notice the talents of these Mastiff–Bulldog–terrier composite dogs. Eager to further develop their own lines, they carefully bred and kept meticulous records. Outside of the fighting ring, these new and improved dogs gained notoriety for their strong, handsome presentation and loyal, affectionate natures with their families.

Yet another modern descendant of the original fighting pit terriers is the Staffordshire Bull Terrier (also known as Staffords or Staffy Bulls). Noticeably smaller than the APBT or AmStaff, the Staffy Bull is an energetic little terrier with lots of charm. It is the most popular terrier breed in England today.

Dog handlers were physically present in the pit during dog fights, acting as referees and coaches. Tolerance and acceptance of humans in the dogs were necessary for owners to train and tend to their fighters, and any aggression toward humans was regarded as a serious defect in an otherwise desirable

APBTs are famous for their handsome appearance and loyal nature.

Breed Club Recognition

- The American Pit Bull Terrier (APBT) — Recognized by the ADBA and UKC.
- The American Staffordshire Terrier (AmStaff or AST) — Recognized by the AKC.
- The Staffordshire Bull Terrier (SBT) — Recognized by the AKC, UKC, and KC.

bloodline.

Americans ventured west, populating the frontier as farmers and ranchers and taking advantage of the large hybrid dogs' superior hunting skills, as well as their suitability as family pets. They began to realize that the dogs were equipped to do more than entertain in blood sports. Careful breeding continued, and by the end of the nineteenth century, the evolving breed resulted in the APBT we know today.

RECOGNITION OF THE APBT

The APBT's unsavory fighting history made the road to recognition difficult in the United States. With good old American ingenuity, though, APBT enthusiasts found their way around the roadblocks keeping the breed in obscurity.

The United Kennel Club (UKC)

Although the breed quickly became popular in America, it wasn't until 1898 that it was officially named the American Pit Bull Terrier. In an attempt to firmly establish this dog as an American breed, dog enthusiast Chauncey Z. Bennett created the United Kennel Club (UKC), with the APBT as its first recognized breed.

A commonly asked question is why the APBT is not recognized by the American Kennel Club (AKC). The fact is that in the late nineteenth century and early twentieth century, the AKC *did* acknowledge the APBT, but the breed name changed, and ultimately, the breed itself.

When the UKC was first created in 1898, its primary concern was recognition and acceptance of APBTs, not dog shows. This frustrated a group of APBT owners who wanted to use the show ring to promote their breed as more than a pit-fighting dog. This group pushed for AKC recognition and won it in 1936, but with one condition—the breed's name would have to be changed. The AKC wouldn't associate itself with any breed with the word "pit" in its name.

The first name considered was "American Bull Terrier," but it was discarded for sounding too similar to the firmly entrenched Bull Terrier Club of the AKC. "Yankee Terrier" was a possibility, but it too was discarded. In an effort to reflect the breed's early ties to Bulldogs and terriers, the name "Staffordshire Terrier" was agreed upon, as such a large part of the Bull Terrier's ancestry came from that part of England. But the name was not popular with some members of the original disgruntled group of American dog owners. They decided to stay with the UKC and keep the original name "American Pit Bull Terrier." In doing so, they forever separated the APBT from the AmStaff.

Today, the APBT is one of the most widely exhibited dogs in the United States, through over 10,000 conformation shows, weight-pulling competitions, and other sporting events sponsored by the UKC.

The first dog of any breed to ever earn quadruple-event UKC titles is—you guessed it—an APBT. Superdog UWP UAGCH UUD CH 'PR' Columbia River Penina Muumu DNA-P OFA, CGC, TT, TC, NJC, owned, trained, and handled by Michael Snyder, has racked up an impressive string of titles since she first began competing in 1998. This beautiful powerhouse has a personal best of 1,130 pounds (512.6 kg) in weight-pulling competition. She has whelped one litter of four puppies, two of which have gone on to become

The APBT is currently one of the most widely exhibited dogs in the United States.

The Endangered Breed Association (EBA)

Another organization created with the APBT in mind, the Endangered Breed Association (EBA), was founded in 1980 by APBT supporter Ralph Greenwood. This nonprofit group's mission is to protect animal breeds that are victims of misunderstanding, controversy, or just plain ignorance. Members strive to educate the public, and when necessary, retain legal aid for innocent victims caught in unfair controversy. The preservation of the APBT is their primary focus, and they work persistently to prevent unjust breed-specific legislation from being enacted.

titleholders themselves. Penina truly is a superdog and a prime example of an APBT with huge potential.

The American Kennel Club (AKC)

Around the time the UKC was founded, in 1898, the American Pit Bull Terrier and the American Staffordshire Terrier (AKC-recognized) were essentially the same dog. The only difference between the two breeds was the name. In fact, the very first American Staffordshire Terrier (AmStaff) registered with the AKC was actually an APBT. "Pete," the mascot of *Little Rascals* fame, was chosen to be the AKC's first official AmStaff. It would take more than half a century of subsequent breeding strictly for conformation purposes to acquire the physical differences between the two breeds.

As mentioned earlier, the AKC finally agreed to accept APBTs for registration in 1936, as long as the breed name was changed. But what to call the APBT? We discussed before that the name "American Bull Terrier" was submitted, but it was too close to the Bull Terrier already established in England and the United States. The Staffordshire Bull Terrier, recognized in England in 1935, was the closest relation to the APBT in America, so it made sense to use a similar name to satisfy the AKC. Thus, APBTs were registered with the AKC as Staffordshire Terriers.

This was fine until the 1970s, when the AKC recognized the British breed Staffordshire Bull Terrier. The latter name was too close for comfort to the Staffordshire Terrier, so the word "American" was added in 1972. The "pit dogs" who became APBTs with the UKC, and Staffordshire Terriers with the AKC, were now known as American Staffordshire Terriers.

The UKC will allow registration of an AmStaff as an APBT, but the AKC will not register an APBT as an AmStaff. This disparity has led to a common misconception that dogs registered with the UKC are somehow inferior to dogs of the same breed registered with the AKC. On the contrary, breeds traditionally considered "UKC breeds," such as the APBT, are of outstanding quality. Breeders attracted to membership in the UKC are serious about preserving breed type and celebrating all its fine qualities, not just physical appearance. How a dog performs the job he has been bred to do is just as important as how closely he matches the established breed standard. For

APBT or AmStaff?

The commonalities of both breeds have made them almost indistinguishable, even to the trained eye. With a few exceptions, the breed standards are almost identical. Two helpful exceptions are nose color and flash (areas of white). The AmStaff standard considers red noses and excessive white coat markings faults. If the dog has a red nose or a coat that is more than one-third white, he's probably an APBT. The APBT stands slightly taller than the AmStaff and is generally more athletic and driven. Both breeds are known to be dog-aggressive, but in the APBT it is slightly stronger and more common. If the dog has uncropped ears, it is an APBT, as the AKC mandates cropped ears on AmStaffs. Both breeds have an infinite capacity for love of their humans, so either way, you come out ahead!

AmStaffs in the show ring, looks are extremely important. For APBTs, both looks and performance are valued, with the emphasis definitely on the latter.

The American Dog Breeders Association (ADBA)

Eleven years after the UKC was founded, another APBT-focused organization was created. The American Dog Breeders Association (ADBA) was established in 1909 by staunch APBT supporter Guy McCord, with the intent of dispelling the impression that the APBT was a dog used only for fighting. This remains an ongoing effort, but the ADBA has greatly contributed to APBT myth busting, and today it is the leading registry for the breed. The Salt Lake City-based group sponsors conformation shows and weight-pulling matches for the only breed it registers—the APBT.

A well-trained APBT is an affectionate and hard-working dog. His strong desire to please his owner—even if that owner wants him to fight—allows him to excel at obedience, agility, and other activities that showcase the breed's intelligence, strength, and trainability. Appreciation and respect for these characteristics make today's APBT a more appealing companion than ever before.

Chapter 2

CHARACTERISTICS
of the American Pit Bull Terrier

No doubt about it—a healthy, happy APBT cuts a handsome figure. With his sleek, shiny coat, intelligent eyes, and well-developed musculature, he is easily one of the best-looking breeds around, and nothing scores higher on the cuteness scale than an exuberant APBT puppy.

It is difficult to reconcile the enthusiastic, intelligent roughneck that is today's APBT with the fearless fighter his ancestors were cultivated to be. This breed would much rather spend his life as a lap dog—albeit a large one—who views the world as his personal playground. Thanks to ongoing education about the breed's true characteristics, in time, his unsavory heritage may no longer precede him. After all, the Bulldog was once bred to fight, but no one would consider the breed inherently vicious today. To promote a more appropriate public image, we need to examine just what the APBT is made of, inside and out.

THE UKC BREED STANDARD

Every recognized dog breed has an official standard that specifically outlines its desired appearance. Written by the national club representing the breed, the standard serves as a blueprint for the ideal specimen. The majority of breed standards are written by affiliate clubs of the American Kennel Club (AKC). In the case of the APBT, who is not acknowledged by the AKC, the United Kennel Club (UKC) has compiled the breed standard with input from national breed associations and top breeders actively solicited for this purpose. Responsible breeders view the breed standard as the pinnacle of excellence and strive to produce dogs who come as close to it as possible.

As mentioned in Chapter 1, the reason for the AKC's exclusion of the APBT goes back to the divergence of the breed in the last century. The APBT was a single breed with two names: American Pit Bull Terrier and American Staffordshire Terrier (AmStaff). The latter was an effort to distance the breed from its unsavory fighting origins, because the AKC did not want to register a breed name containing the word "pit." At first, the organization agreed to register APBTs as AmStaffs, even though it was not a different breed. A handful of APBT purists resisted this movement and opted not to register with the AKC at all, intead registering with the UKC. Subsequent breeding produced distinct differences between the APBT and the AmStaff, and the two breeds forever separated.

Head

Medium length. Brick-like in shape. Skull flat and widest at the ears, with prominent cheeks free from wrinkles.

The head offers the first impression of the overall appearance of the dog and should give the APBT a chiseled look. His muzzle is more elongated than that of his Boxer and Bulldog cousins, making breathing easier. Pendulous jowls were a

Reasons for Human Aggression in APBTs

While rare, human aggression can occur in APBTs, usually for the following reasons:

- Some people like the "status" of owning a dangerous or vicious dog. A friendly little pup may be encouraged by an unscrupulous owner to display aggression toward people. The eager-to-please APBT will be just as mean as his owner wants him to be.

- Unreasonable or harsh discipline can spark anxiety in a dog and cause him to bite out of fear. The only acceptable means of discipline for any dog is positive reinforcement.

- Dogs are social animals. Neglect and isolation will prevent a happy puppy's personality from thriving. He may become timid, aloof, or ornery. An APBT who doesn't interact much with humans may feel threatened and defensive.

detriment to the fighting pit dog of yesteryear and have been bred out. The APBT's facial skin fits smoothly and tightly over the protruding muscle.

Muzzle

Square, wide, and deep. Well-pronounced jaws, displaying strength. Upper teeth should meet tightly over lower teeth, outside in front.

The angles of the APBT's jaw converge slightly, so they are not as square as those of a Boxer. The prominent underjaw should give the impression of a square muzzle. An improperly formed lower jaw will give the impression of a pointy muzzle and detracts from his powerful appearance. The lips should fit tightly over the jaws, and the upper front teeth should fit tightly outside the lower front teeth in a *scissors bite*. This is the strongest bite a dog can have and the best for gripping.

The APBT's head should be medium in length and brick-like in shape.

Substandard bites fall into one of three types: *undershot*, where the lower jaw protrudes so that the lower front teeth close in front of the upper incisors; *overshot*, where the upper jaw protrudes so that there is a gap between the upper and lower front teeth when the dog's mouth is closed; and the rarer *wry* bite, which is a scissors bite on one side but undershot on the other. Most faulty bites are cosmetic in nature and have no impact on the dog's quality of life.

Ears

Cropped or uncropped. Should be set high on head and be free from wrinkles.

Ear cropping is the subject of controversy around the world, largely because there is no medical reason for it. Contrary to some belief, uncropped or natural ears are no more susceptible to ear afflictions than cropped ears. In dog fighting's heyday, APBT's ears were cropped not only to give them a fiercer appearance but also to eliminate the risk of injury. Natural ears were an easy jaw hold for the opposing dog, and torn ears bled profusely.

Today, the practice of ear cropping is banned in several countries around the world. If you choose to have your APBT's ears cropped, find a veterinarian experienced with the breed, as the prick-eared look is different from that of a Boxer or Doberman Pinscher. When cropped properly, prick ears should stand up on their own with little or no "training" period.

The APBT's natural ears are fairly small and classified as either *rose* or *half-prick*. Rose ears fold slightly backward, exposing a little of the inner ear. The tips usually point toward the side, but sometimes they point backward, depending on their size, formation, and whether or not the dog is resting or responding to a stimulus. Half-pricked ears start upward, then flop forward about halfway up. They are closer to the front of the dog's head than rose ears. Occasionally, an APBT will have fully drooping ears like those of a spaniel. These

Natural ears are no more susceptible to ear afflictions than cropped ears.

are nonstandard but function no differently than any other ears.

Eyes

Round. Should be set far apart, low down on skull. Any color acceptable.

Eyes set closely together are considered a cosmetic fault and tend to give the APBT a crafty rather than intelligent expression. They also make the muzzle appear too narrow and long, depriving the APBT of the bold look so characteristic of the breed. A quick way to evaluate properly set eyes is to see if the outside corner of the eye is in line with the indentation directly over the beginning of the cheek muscle. If so, the eyes are set at the most attractive height relative to the skull. Eye colors ranging from brown to green are acceptable; blue eyes are considered a serious fault, but they do not disqualify the dog from competition.

Nose

Wide-open nostrils. Any color acceptable.

We don't often think of dogs' noses varying in color, but they do. Picture a reddish-brown nose, reddish-fawn coat, and green eyes. Beautiful!

Neck

Muscular. Slightly arched. Tapering from shoulder to head. Free from looseness of skin.

Good musculature emphasizes a nicely arched neck, so the APBT's neck should appear strong. The neck should be narrowest just behind the ears, gradually widening downward to blend into the top of the shoulders (withers). Tightly fitting skin is desirable on an APBT, so any hanging skin under the throat is a cosmetic fault.

Shoulders

Strong and muscular, with wide, sloping shoulder blades.

The shoulder blade should have an obvious backward slope from its lower end (at the dog's upper arm) to its higher end (just in front of the withers). Properly sloped shoulders are often called *well laid back*. Shoulders lacking proper slope are called *straight* or *upright shoulders* and are undesirable. By limiting the

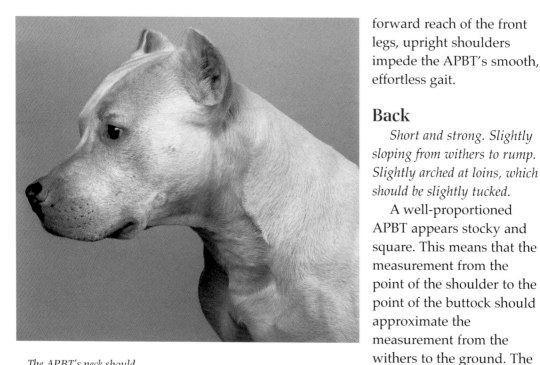

The APBT's neck should appear muscular and feature tightly fitting skin.

forward reach of the front legs, upright shoulders impede the APBT's smooth, effortless gait.

Back

Short and strong. Slightly sloping from withers to rump. Slightly arched at loins, which should be slightly tucked.

A well-proportioned APBT appears stocky and square. This means that the measurement from the point of the shoulder to the point of the buttock should approximate the measurement from the withers to the ground. The topline, or area from the top of the back from the withers to where the tail begins, should be wrinkle free and smooth.

Some topline faults are mild enough to be mainly cosmetic, but some structural problems can weaken the back and hinder proper gait. A *soft* or *dip* topline is one of the most common issues and gives a swaybacked appearance. *Roach back* is a topline fault in which the spine arches in a convex curve beginning from behind the withers and becoming very pronounced above the loins. An APBT who is *high in the rear* has a back that is higher in the croup (where the tail begins) than at the withers and is considered faulty.

The loin area is the APBT's waistline. It should have a pronounced indentation when viewed from above that makes the dog appear slim but not weak.

Chest

Deep but not too broad, with wide-sprung ribs.

The APBT should have a space between his front legs wide enough to accommodate a well-developed *brisket*, or forechest. It should be deep enough at its lowest point to be even with the dog's elbow when viewed from the side. If the brisket is too broad, though, the APBT will be less agile and look more like a Bulldog.

Ribs

Close. Well-sprung, with deep-back ribs.

When an APBT's rib cage continues far back toward the hindquarters, the back is considered *well ribbed* or *deep in the rear*. This is a plus because deep-back ribs allow more room for lung expansion during exercise, thereby increasing his stamina.

How can you tell if an APBT is lacking in depth of rib? If room is available for more than the width of a human's hand between the last rib and the thigh, the dog's ribs are nonconforming.

Tail

Short in comparison to size. Set low and tapering to a fine point. Not carried over back. Bobbed tail not acceptable.

The APBT's long, slender tail is a continuation of the spinal column and should be just as strong and well formed, beginning with a thick root that tapers to a point. When in motion, the APBT should not carry his tail any higher than the top of his back. High-carried or curled tails are faulty.

Unlike that of Boxers or Doberman Pinschers, the APBT breed standard does not require tail docking. This was not done even in fighting days, because the tail was rarely involved during fights. (Dogs instinctively targeted the opponent's throat and surrounding area.) The APBT should proudly carry the tail with which he was born.

Legs

Large, round boned, with straight, upright pasterns, reasonably strong. Feet to be of medium size. Gait should be light and springy. No rolling or pacing.

The leg bones should appear to easily support the dog's weight. An APBT who looks like a log held up by four toothpicks is cosmetically and structurally faulty. Feet should point directly frontward, neither toward each other nor away from each other. Feet that point anywhere other than toward the front may indicate weak *pasterns*. (A pastern is the part of the leg from the joint just above the foot down to the foot.)

Foot size should be appropriate to the overall size of the

A long, slender tail is a defining characteristic of the APBT.

APBT. Feet that stand out as being too large or too small are faulty, as are flat feet and splayed feet.

The APBT's gait should appear smooth and effortless, with a jaunty air of confidence. There should be no rolling from side to side or *pacing* (occurring when a dog's front and rear legs on the same side move forward together). The correct gait for an APBT is a trot, a diagonal gait where the left front and the right rear legs move forward together, followed by the counterparts.

Thigh

Long, with muscles developed. Hocks down and straight.

The rear leg has an upper thigh and a lower thigh, separated by a knee joint called the *stifle*. Both sections of thigh should be strong and well muscled.

The *hock joint* is the joint between the stifle and the foot. An APBT's hock should be located closer to the ground than it is to the middle of his rear leg. This is called *hocks down*.

Viewed from the rear, the back legs should appear parallel. Faulty hocks will turn in toward each other or away from each other.

Coat

Glossy. Short and stiff to the touch.

The sleek, velvety coat has somewhat coarse-textured hairs that provide optimal protection for a shorthaired dog. A shiny, beautiful coat is the hallmark of prime health and condition of an APBT.

Color

Any color and most markings permissible.

Typical colors include black, fawn, red, chocolate brown, and white. Striped patterns on a background color are called *brindle* and can be in any color combination. Dogs with areas of white (called *flash*) on a colored background are described as flashy red or flashy brindle. The only unacceptable color is a spotty, patchy coloration called *merle*. Merle coloration results from a dilution gene that lightens whatever the coat color would otherwise have been. The lightening is not spread evenly over the coat but leaves scatterings of undiluted color over the dog's body. Merle puppies are frequently born blind, deaf, or both, so breeding a merle APBT is not in the breed's best interest.

Weight

Not important, as long as in proportion to height. Females preferred from 30 (13.6 kg) to 50 pounds (22.7kg). Males from 35 (15.9 kg) to 60 pounds (27.2 kg).

Today's APBTs are medium-sized dogs who are generally larger than their pit-fighting ancestors. Some of the most renowned fighters weighed less than 35 pounds (15.9 kg), giving rise to the motto, "It's not the size of the dog in the fight; it's the size of the fight in the dog." On the flip side, APBTs have been bred as large as 100 pounds (45.4 kg), but this is a rare occurrence.

Large or small, all APBTs seem to think they are the perfect size for human laps and will gladly make use of yours.

BEHAVIORAL AND PERSONALITY TRAITS

To understand what an APBT is, you must first understand what he is *not*. By now, you know that the APBT is not a vicious man-eater who randomly attacks people with no provocation. In reality, this dog has more virtues than a Boy Scout. He has the uncanny ability to differentiate between friend and foe, making

Typical coat colors include black, fawn, red, chocolate brown, and white.

him a natural guardian. He is able to display anger in one direction and affection in the other repeatedly, without misdirecting the aggression.

Still, the APBT is not a one-size-fits-all breed. He has distinct inclinations and needs that must be carefully examined before making the decision to add him to your family. With a little homework, you will be able to tell if you and an APBT are destined for each other.

Temperament

By nature, the APBT is an affectionate, anxious-to-please dog, but most people never hear that. Any publicity the breed gets is usually negative, including injuries to humans or other pets and proposed legislation banning "pit bulls." Even if a confrontation is not the APBT's fault, the fact that a "pit bull" is involved will surely headline the news item.

Would you be surprised to learn that properly bred, socialized, and trained APBTs are among the *least* likely dogs to be human-aggressive? Remember, when dog fighting was in its heyday during the last century, dog handlers acted as referees and coaches during fights, right there in the pits with the dogs. Handlers bathed their opponents' dogs prior to each fight to make sure no poisonous substance was applied to the fur. All this would have been impossible if the dogs were aggressive toward humans.

Gameness

Ask any APBT fan what the breed's most prominent trait is, and the answer will likely be gameness. *Gameness* means the willingness of a dog to continue his task—whether it is fighting, hunting, cart pulling, or defending his human—through great stress and pain, even until death. Early bullfighting dogs were known to go back to the bull with broken legs and stomachs ripped open.

Gameness has nothing to do with viciousness or bravery; it has to do with heart. An APBT will keep on keeping on, no matter what he encounters. This do-or-die attitude would be admired in an NFL quarterback, but when applied to the APBT, it is misconstrued as dangerous.

APBT Temperament

By nature, the APBT is an affectionate, anxious-to-please dog.

Strength

The APBT's power and strength are the result of more than a century of survival under dreadful circumstances. Descendants of the fighting dogs who thrived in the direst situations emerged as kings of the evolving dog sport of weight pulling. Pound for pound, the APBT is an incredibly strong dog in a relatively small package. Constant control must be maintained at all times with even the friendliest APBT—perhaps *because* of his extreme friendliness. Unchecked exuberance could easily overpower an unsuspecting handler, even if the dog is exhibiting nonaggressive excitement. That is why proper socialization and training are musts for these powerhouses.

Human Aggression

It bears repeating: A properly bred and trained APBT is *less* likely to bite humans than other dog breeds or mixes. In fact, the APBT's trusting and friendly nature has enabled strangers to enter yards, unchain him, and walk away with him.

Why, then, is it always a "pit bull" who attacks a child and makes the evening news? Because the term "pit bull" is a misnomer. The child's attacker is probably not an APBT but some untrained derivation or mixed breed. Or it might not be

APBTs are known for their strength and tenacity.

either; it may be just a mongrel dubbed a "pit bull" by unenlightened journalists chasing the sensational. A child bitten by a dog isn't news—a child bitten by a "pit bull" is.

Dog Aggression

While APBTs are not aggressive toward humans, they can be antagonistic toward other dogs. This may be a negative trait, but it is a trait that warrants discussion. Remember that the original purpose of the terrier as a dog group was to combat rodents and other animals. These instincts are not easily diffused just because modern science has eradicated the need for such dog jobs. Many breeds are dog-aggressive, but a squabble between an APBT and another breed of dog has more serious connotations than a confrontation between, say, a Chihuahua and that same breed. The good news is that any dog, even the breeds considered most dog-aggressive, can learn to ignore other animals and avoid confrontation.

Loyalty and Companionability

Far from the menacing beast he is often portrayed as, the APBT makes a loving, trusting, entertaining pet. He enjoys being with his humans and will devote his life to serving them. He is good-natured with children and very tolerant of their accidental roughness. A high tolerance for pain means that the accidental tail pull or toe step by a young child won't faze the APBT. He will play for hours with his human children, often sensing which ones are too young for extreme rough-and-tumble play. He is a master at discerning when to show affection and does not misdirect aggression. This makes the APBT a natural, competent guardian—a protector, not a perpetrator.

IS AN APBT RIGHT FOR YOU?

The decision to add a pet to your family should always be a conscious, educated one. This is doubly true when you're thinking of acquiring an APBT. Potential owners must ask themselves several questions to see if the breed fits their lifestyle, and vice versa. You should know what challenges you and the APBT will face, and how you will deal with them.

Environment

APBTs are energetic dogs who require a good deal of regular, hard exercise, so it makes sense to question if your environment is suited to the breed.

The ideal situation for an APBT is a house with a fenced-in yard—a real fence, not an electronic barrier. Invisible fences are not infallible, and a determined APBT will put up with a brief electric shock if temptation calls from outside the fenced area. If you don't have a real fence and cannot put one up, early obedience training is crucial so that you never lose control of your APBT. Also, supervise him at all times during outdoor playtime, even after he is trained.

Common sense says that large or highly active dog breeds are not the best choices for city pets. Space can be at a premium, sometimes leaving the active APBT with no outlet for all that pent-up energy. If you live in an apartment or in an urban area, it is important that you find a suitable place to take your APBT every day for some quality exercise. Given the APBT's tendency toward

Questions to Ask Yourself Before Becoming an APBT Owner

Ask yourself the following questions before you commit to caring for an APBT:

- *Am I willing to be a public relations representative for this breed?* Questions and comments of all kinds inevitably follow where an APBT leads, so you want to make sure you have the inclination and the patience to debunk the junk.
- *Do I have the resources to invest in the socialization and training of my APBT?* If you don't have the sufficient time and money required to perform these duties, get a different breed.
- *Can I afford to purchase a quality APBT?* When it comes to this breed, you don't want a bargain-basement dog with a dubious background. The peace of mind you pay for in a well-bred APBT is worth the extra money.
- *Have I thoroughly familiarized myself with the breed and evaluated my suitability for APBT ownership?* If you have done all your homework and honestly feel you can do right by this breed, congratulations. You are on your way to a rewarding relationship!

dog aggression, a dog park isn't an ideal solution unless it has individual runs where you can prevent contact with other dogs.

At the same time, there are ways to make sure the city APBT stays active. If you're a jogger with a well-trained and socialized APBT, take him with you for an after-work run. Surf the Internet to see if other APBT owners with the same concerns live in your city. If their dogs are well trained, too, you can schedule "play dates."

Although the breed is generally better off in a suburban or rural setting, many rescued or adopted APBTs live happily in the big city. A loving home in any setting is better than a neglectful owner who views the dog as a commodity.

APBTs and Children

Young children must be supervised until they are old enough to understand how to gently interact with a dog. As stated before, APBTs are so docile around children that they will endure inadvertent pummeling and pulling. But by the same token, care must be taken that a child does not interfere with a dog who is eating, and a toddler should never try to take away a toy from a dog. It is never too early for children to be taught never to tease or mistreat a dog or any animal.

APBTs are docile around children, but young children must be closely supervised until they understand how to interact with them properly.

Exercise Requirements

High-energy APBTs require an outlet for their enthusiasm. Vigorous daily exercise benefits both the dog and his human and should be scheduled as a regular activity. This means that the APBT may not be the ideal pet for the elderly or for the family whose schedule doesn't allow for quality time with the dog.

Leash walking is an acceptable mode of exercise, provided you are strong enough to control the dog if he starts to pull. When he does, you can expect to be swept off your feet. Your strength is no match for his, which is

Children and Dogs: Important Points to Learn

To keep your child safe around dogs, teach her the following points:

- Strange dogs should be approached with the same caution as strange humans.
- Never run up to or chase an unfamiliar dog. He may feel threatened and bite.
- Never bother a dog who is eating, and never attempt to take away his food.
- Do not take a dog's toy away while he is playing with it.
- When meeting a new dog, ask his owner if you may pet him. If given the green light, hold out a closed fist for him to sniff, which is less threatening than an open hand. A dog startled by an open hand thrust at his face might snap at the fingers.

why he must learn to obey you. Encounters with unfamiliar humans and dogs most often take place on leash walks, and full control of your APBT is of the utmost importance.

What is the best form of exercise for your APBT? Almost anything goes. An outdoor game or structured activity gives the dog quality time with you while using his power and strength to their best advantage. Try hanging an old tire on a rope from a tree. APBTs can busy themselves with this for hours, play biting and jumping for the tire. Tetherball makes another lively game for the whole family, including your APBT.

Whether it's organized canine sports or spontaneous games in the backyard, what matters is that your APBT is getting a great workout while having fun.

Adding any dog to your family is an exciting event to anticipate, but not something to be undertaken lightly. It requires careful consideration, commitment, and preparation.

Obtaining an APBT on a whim can turn what should be a happy time into a nightmare, and it is not fair to your family or to the dog. To bring out the best in an APBT, you must bring out the best in yourself as his teacher, caregiver, and companion. Once you have committed to providing him with the time, love, and care he needs to thrive, your emotional investment will be returned a hundredfold.

PREPARING
for Your American Pit Bull Terrier

reparing properly for your APBT's arrival is one of the most important things you can do for him. First, you must decide what kind of puppy you are looking for and where to purchase or adopt him. Then, you need to consider what necessities he will need to make a smooth adjustment to his new position in your family. Nutritious puppy food, safe and age-appropriate toys, a comfortably appointed dog crate, and the phone number of a trusted veterinarian are all things that should be in place well before your new APBT arrives. You will also want to puppy-proof your home, removing anything that poses a safety hazard to the newest family member. In addition, you'll want to purchase some cleaning supplies in anticipation of the accidents your dog will surely have. A little advance planning goes a long way toward minimizing the stress of this significant lifestyle change. Your APBT will be with you a long time, and your commitment to keeping him happy and healthy requires some effort.

PRELIMINARY DECISIONS

Before you get your heart set on adding an APBT to your family, first make sure no legislative stumbling blocks exist. Unfortunately, some areas have restrictions on the ownership of certain "vicious" breeds; find out if yours is one of them. Once you get the green light to purchase or adopt an APBT, it's important to look at the big picture and clarify your expectations from your pet. Do you want a companion who will accompany the family on day trips and outings? Do you want your pet to participate in one of the many organized activities for dogs, or more specifically, for APBTs? Do you plan to become involved in the breeding community? Do you have a preference for a male dog over female, or vice versa? What traits, if any, are gender specific? Having a clear vision for the future with your APBT will enable you to select the right dog from the right source.

Puppy Versus Adult

One important decision you have to make is whether an APBT puppy or adult is the best fit for you and your family. People generally prefer a puppy when adding a dog to the family, and who can blame them? Few things in this world are more endearing. Bringing a puppy to your home presents its own distinct requirements, though. You must be mentally and practically ready to deal with housetraining, teething, puppy-proofing your living space, and the puppy's transition from communal litter to independence. In many ways, puppies demand the same commitment as human babies, and for a while, your world will revolve around his adjustment and well-being. This temporary, high-maintenance phase is well compensated by the sheer joy a pet brings. A puppy is essentially a clean slate. He has little or no previous

Do your research before deciding whether a puppy or adult is right for you.

ownership and no bad habits to unlearn. This means that proper training will rest completely on your shoulders, and it is up to you to see that it is done right.

What if you'd rather skip the work and disruption involved during puppyhood? An adult dog may be the happy solution. There are always adult dogs in need of a new home, for a variety of reasons. APBT adoption or rescue can save one more homeless dog from euthanasia. But remember that adult dogs may have issues of their own, depending on their circumstances. Adopting an adult APBT doesn't guarantee smooth sailing. Find out as much as you can about an adult APBT's background before accepting him.

Did You Know?

Spaying or castrating your dog is not an option if you want to breed your APBT and/or participate in conformation shows.

Male Versus Female

If you are undecided about the sex of your future pet and seek input from the owners of APBTs of both sexes, you will likely get several different opinions. Some say females are more easily trained and form a closer bond with their owners. Others maintain that male dogs have more character and a more consistent temperament. At the end of the day, personality and character are subjective and vary from dog to dog.

Regardless of gender, you must consider neutering your APBT. If companionship is your primary motivation in getting a dog, it's a good idea to neuter. By removing the sexual hormones, you spare yourself the inconvenience of twice yearly estrus cycles in females and the more dominant nature of an intact male. Both sexes tend to be somewhat calmer when altered. Bear in mind that the veterinary bill will be higher for spaying than for castration.

If you want to breed your APBT and/or participate in conformation shows, spaying or castrating is not an option. Be prepared to have some extra patience when training your intact male, and educate yourself on potential health issues that pertain to intact bitches, such as false pregnancy and uterine cancer.

Show- Versus Pet-Quality APBTs

So you go to pick out the APBT pup you want to add to your family, but the breeder says she's keeping that one to show. She points out the other available pups in the litter who are "pet quality" but not show worthy. Are you getting an inferior dog here? Not at all. It is a misconception to think that any puppy who isn't show quality is somehow inferior to his littermates in terms of temperament or health. The breeder merely rules out pet-quality pups as conformation show contenders. It's hard for non-show people to comprehend how breeders can foretell a future showstopper. The physical imperfections they see in pet-quality puppies go unnoticed by the untrained eye. You just want a healthy, loving pet; do you really care if your APBT isn't a sterling example of the breed standard? Of course not. The breeder will probably require you to neuter your pet-quality APBT (something responsible pet owners do anyway), ensuring that the puppy's "faults" will not be passed down to future generations. Pet-quality dogs have the added appeal of a lower price tag than their show-bound littermates.

WHERE TO FIND THE APBT OF YOUR DREAMS

Dogs come into their humans' lives in many ways. People adopt from animal shelters, they rehabilitate rescued dogs, and they buy from breeders. Sometimes dogs find their humans, and these humans become the adopted ones. Often the dogs' histories are mysteries.

But if it's an APBT you want, you absolutely must know what you're getting. You need to be sure of your source's integrity, and you need to be aware that a rescued or adopted

Bringing Your Puppy Home

There's no way around it—puppies are work. Most people find the rewards well worth the temporary inconvenience, but it makes sense to plan ahead for the tumultuous first days.

As exciting as a new pet is, remember what the puppy is experiencing. He has been taken away from the comfort and companionship of his mother and littermates, as well as the familiarity of his breeder. He doesn't know yet about the love you will shower on him; he only knows that he is in a strange environment. Create a soothing, peaceful atmosphere for homecoming day. Plan to bring the puppy home when the family can devote the whole day to him. If possible, take some time off work.

A puppy may be a popular holiday gift, but holidays are not the time to bring one home. Even happy confusion can be overwhelming, and your routine will be unclear. Likewise, don't go away on vacation right after your puppy comes home. The first weeks with you represent crucial bonding time, and he will feel insecure if you leave him in someone else's care so soon.

APBT of questionable heritage may have an unpredictable temperament. If you answer an ad for "pit bulls," understand that you're taking a risk and possibly setting yourself up for a lot of heartache.

The personality and character of an APBT vary from dog to dog.

Responsible APBT ownership is not for the fainthearted. It requires knowledge, loving patience, and material resources. Get started on the right foot by researching the best way to bring a wonderful APBT into your life.

Breeders

One wonderful source from which to acquire a purebred dog is a reputable breeder. Never has this been more important than with the APBT. You want to be certain of your dog's heritage before you buy, ensuring that he is a true APBT and not a melting pot of similar "bully breed" combinations with unknown physical and temperamental histories. If you have decided to adopt an adult dog, APBT breeders are still the best place to begin your search. Although breeders most often sell puppies, they may have adults in need of good homes. This doesn't mean anything is wrong with the dog. Sometimes a lifestyle change ultimately forces a buyer to relinquish his dog, or perhaps a puppy owner discovered that the special responsibility of APBT ownership was more than she bargained for. Most breeders would rather have the adult dog returned to them than dropped off at the nearest animal shelter. It is much better that a dog in this situation be returned to the breeder instead of remaining in an unsuitable home.

How to Find a Reputable Breeder

How do you go about finding a reputable APBT breeder? By going right to the source. A quick Internet search will instantly provide a wealth of information on where and how to locate a breeder. The websites of the UKC and ADBA can point you toward the nearest APBT club. Trade publications such as the UKC's *Bloodlines* or the ADBA's *American Pit Bull Terrier Gazette* feature ads of APBT litters and dogs at stud. Mainstream magazines like *Dog Fancy* and *Dog World* also have extensive breeder listings.

Networking is always a good supplement to any search. Let other dog owners know that you are looking for a reputable APBT breeder. Even if they don't know of any, they might know someone else who does, perhaps an American Staffordshire Terrier or Staffordshire Bull Terrier breeder who can direct you to an APBT kennel. Just be sure to limit your networking to those who understand what a true APBT is.

What to Look for

When you visit a breeder from whom you may purchase a dog, let your instincts be your guide. Is the kennel clean and the dogs happy and well cared for? Is at least one

Backyard Breeders

Not all breeders are created equal. It's important to remember that casual or "backyard" breeders are not the best choice when shopping for an APBT. At best, they have good intentions when it comes to the puppies' well-being, but these people aren't familiar with the lineage of their bitch or the stud dog she mated with. And although the backyard breeder might be vigilant about finding the best homes for her pups, you may not be purchasing a top-quality pet.

At all costs, avoid breeders who randomly breed their dogs, looking to make a buck on the sale of puppies. These people have no interest in responsible breeding and little or no information on heritage. A puppy obtained from this kind of breeder is a huge risk, because you have no clue about his parents' temperaments or medical histories. The dogs may be advertised as APBTs, when in fact they may be any kind of reasonable facsimile.

A breeder's puppies should appear happy, active, and well cared for.

parent on the premises? You should be able to get a feeling for what kind of breeder you are dealing with, but you should also look for the following:

- participation in some kind of organized dog activity or sport
- references from other clients
- the desire to advance the APBT breed, not to make money
- willingness to take back the dog you buy if at any time during the dog's life, you must give him up for any reason
- willingness to provide a pedigree chart on your pup going back three generations
- does not breed in high volume, where multiple bitches are pregnant at the same time, or breed one litter right after another
- asks thorough questions about your home environment, lifestyle, feeding style, security, and anything that may impact your new dog
- a genuine love of APBTs and concern for their welfare

Adoption

With so many millions of homeless dogs around the world, adoption seems logical and ethical. Like everything, it has its pros and cons. True APBTs are rarely up for adoption; more prevalent are APBT look-alikes of questionable heritage. You may not know what happened to the dog prior to the adoption, and past misfortunes have a great impact on future behavior. You just don't know. And a "pit bull" with an unpredictable

Adopting an adult APBT is a loving choice that will change his life.

temperament is potentially dangerous.

Certainly, not all adoptees are bad news. Extenuating circumstances that have nothing to do with the APBT may require a new home for a perfectly good dog. Perhaps an APBT's family is relocating to an area with anti-breed legislation. The death of an owner might leave an APBT an orphan. A breeder may have a young adult who did not grow into the show dog she hoped for. These people would be thrilled to find loving adoptive homes for their dogs.

If you can resist the siren call of puppyhood, adopting an adult APBT is a loving choice. Your local animal shelter is always worth a look, but it is unlikely that they will have true APBTs. Any "pit bull" they have is probably a mixed breed of dubious heritage. At any rate, because many county and state laws require automatic euthanasia of any pit dog seized from unprincipled owners, the number of "pit bulls" available for adoption at a shelter will be small.

On the other hand, the United States has many APBT rescue organizations clamoring for foster and permanent homes for the dogs they save from abuse and neglect. Be aware, though, that a rescued APBT will probably have behavioral issues. Commitment and patience are prerequisites for appropriate adoptive families. But remember that at the end of the road to rehabilitation is a loyal, loving dog who will be eternally grateful for your kindness.

Finding a Reputable Shelter or Rescue

The best resource for finding a shelter or APBT rescue organization is the Internet. The ASPCA, UKC, and your local humane society should also be able to connect you with shelters in your area. Keep in mind that some shelters won't accept pit dogs of unknown heritage. If you are looking to adopt an APBT, do an Internet search for "APBT rescue," and you will find lots of helpful information.

What to Look For

Pay a visit to the animal shelter you are considering, just as you would a breeder. Consider the following:

- Are the facilities clean and not too crowded?
- Is the staff compassionate and caring?
- Are they a no-kill (will not euthanize unadopted animals) or low-kill (euthanizes unadopted animals only after a certain time period) shelter?
- Is the shelter or rescue organization recommended by area veterinarians and breeders? Can they put you in touch with others who have adopted from their shelter or rescue?

Networking is a great tool; make use of it.

Internet Source
The best resource for finding a shelter or APBT rescue organization is the Internet.

Pet Stores

Some people decide to buy an APBT from a pet store. Pet stores can be a convenient option, and they usually offer a wide selection of puppies. Remember, however, that a dog's health, happiness, and well-being are largely dependent on his genetics and the quality of his early care. This is why you must ask the pet store to provide you with all the details of the APBT's breeding and history. In fact, pet store employees should be knowledgeable about dogs in general and the breeds they sell in particular.

If you are considering an APBT from a pet store, check the dog for any signs of poor health. A few signs of illness are nasal discharge, watery eyes, and diarrhea. A store should not be selling a dog experiencing any of these symptoms. Even if the puppy seems healthy, be sure to have him checked by your veterinarian as soon as possible. Many health guarantees offered by pet stores are contingent upon a veterinary examination within a few days of the sale.

Questions to Ask Before Purchasing a Pet-Store Puppy

You should ask some of the following questions of pet store personnel before committing to a sale:

1. What kind of guarantee do you offer?

If the store only guarantees the puppy for a few hours or days and offers no compensation for future problems, such as genetic diseases, be aware that you will be on your own to deal with these problems. The store should be reasonably responsible for ensuring you receive a healthy puppy.

2. How old was the puppy when he arrived in the store?

Puppies taken away from their mother and littermates before eight weeks of age are at a great developmental disadvantage. Puppies learn a lot about social interaction from their mother and littermates, and getting shipped across the country in a crate is no way to begin life as a six-week-old puppy. Those taken away too young and exposed to these frightening experiences often develop fearful or aggressive behaviors later in life. The best-case scenario is one in which the puppy was hand delivered by a breeder to a pet store after eight weeks of age.

3. Can I see the vaccination and worming record?

Puppies should have had at least one and preferably two sets of complete vaccinations and a worming by eight weeks. (This can also depend on the breed.) The pet store should have complete documentation of this and any other veterinary care the dogs have received.

4. Is the puppy registered?

Registration is no guarantee of quality, and some registries will register any dog without proof of a pedigree (a written record of a dog's lineage). APBTs who are registered with the UKC may be more likely to come from breeders who are following certain standards, but it's not a guarantee.

Some small local breeders may provide to pet stores puppies who are unregistered but who could make healthy, fine pets. Ask about this, because it will help get the employees talking about the dog and the breeder. The more questions you ask about the store's source for puppies, the more you might be able to find out about the breeder's priorities and history.

CHOOSING THE RIGHT APBT FOR YOU

Before you choose an APBT—puppy or adult—bone up on the breed. If you know someone with an APBT, pick her brain a little. Look at photos of APBTs who are good examples of the breed standard, and talk to local vets for guidance. Don't be shy about arming yourself with information when you choose an APBT.

Physical Appearance

When searching for the perfect APBT, bring along a copy of the breed standard or some pictures for comparison. Do the breeder's APBTs resemble the ones in the photos? Does the APBT you are considering have well-trimmed toenails, a shiny coat, bright eyes, and high energy, all indications of good care? Have neglect or abuse taken a toll on the dog's health, and are you prepared to meet his special needs? Has the APBT had a recent vet checkup? Shots? Wormings? Is the dog clean and parasite free? Ask to see the dog's hip dysplasia certificate. The more you find out up front, the better equipped you will be to make good decisions.

Temperament

A dog's physical condition is often reflected in his disposition. A healthy APBT should be happy just to be alive and eager to make your acquaintance. A sad-looking, introverted dog may not be in good health, and you need to investigate. However, even healthy dogs can exhibit characteristics that are undesirable, like human aggression, severe shyness, and

The APBT whom you are considering should have a shiny coat, bright eyes, and lots of energy.

instability—traits you don't want in your APBT. Some potential owners may think a shy APBT will make an easier, quieter pet, but a timid dog is actually higher maintenance. He will be easily frightened and may become overly dependent on his humans. He could turn into a fear-biter.

Look for a dog who is a happy combination of enthusiasm and malleability. Ask the ABPT breeder to see the temperament test report on the litter's parents, and watch how the dog interacts with other dogs on the premises. Is he getting along fine, or are aggression or shyness issues present? An APBT who has been well socialized will not act frightened around people and other dogs, and he won't try to show dominance over a human.

PAPERWORK

It seems that everything important in our lives involves paperwork, and owning an APBT is no exception. Keeping organized records is the easiest way to manage information essential to your dog's well-being.

A conscientious APBT source will have a packet of information for you when you bring your puppy home. This will include a sales receipt, basic information on the puppy (birth date, color, sex, etc.), medical history (first shots, worming), certificates of registration and health, family tree, feeding instructions, and any other pertinent information, such as veterinarian referrals, books on training, and recommended toys.

From the sales agreement to the health history at the vet to the internment contract with the pet cemetery, life with your APBT will require keeping track of some important documents.

Health Records

Your APBT's collection of health records begins with a certification from the vet that your newly acquired puppy

What to Look for in a Healthy Puppy

The following are some factors that will help you determine whether the APBT you are considering is healthy and well bred.

- Does the puppy look healthy? Is his coat shiny and even? Are his eyes bright and clear?
- Does he act confident and outgoing? A timid, fearful puppy who hangs back from the rest of the litter may exhibit behavioral issues later on.
- Is he more aggressive than exuberant? An overly aggressive puppy may not get along well with other dogs when he matures.
- Has he had the necessary shots and wormings?
- Has he received any socialization?
- Have both parents been fully evaluated for health, temperament, and conformation standards?

is free of infection and contagious diseases, including rabies. This important document not only assures you of a healthy puppy, but it is required information if your puppy travels by air to his new home. You will also need it later on to enroll in obedience classes or board the dog at a kennel.

The health certificate should also indicate the dates of his first DHLPP (distemper, hepatitis, leptospirosis, parvovirus, parainfluenza) shot and subsequent vaccinations. Depending on how old your APBT is when he goes home with you, he may not have received all the required shots. Documents should indicate what shots are still needed and when they should be administered.

A dog's physical condition is sometimes reflected in his disposition.

When you purchase your puppy, make sure that you receive health and temperament certifications of both parents. Look for an Orthopedic Foundation for Animals (OFA) certification that hip dysplasia is not present in the bloodline.

Registration Papers

Because the American Kennel Club (AKC) does not recognize the APBT, registration will be with the United Kennel Club (UKC). A likely scenario is that both parents of an APBT litter will already be registered with the UKC, and the breeder of the puppy will have gone ahead and registered the litter. The registration certificate will be included in your documents packet, and after you have purchased the puppy, you can then notify the UKC of the puppy's new owners and contact information.

New registration of a single APBT is a bit trickier. Like the AKC, the UKC is a "club of clubs" in that it is made up of breed clubs around the country. The UKC normally authorizes single-dog registrations only with the approval of the national breed club affiliate. The breed club may have certain conditions (like requiring performance tests or hip dysplasia clearance) that they feel are in the breed's best interest.

Pedigree

In addition to a registration certificate, a UKC-registered dog owner will receive a three-generation pedigree at no extra charge. What is a pedigree, you may be wondering? It is a chart depicting a dog's ancestors, important for serious show competitors who want champions in their bloodline. The pedigree lists individual dog names, coat colors, and production records (listing who begat whom), useful information for breeders who want to preserve APBT function, structure, and conformation qualities.

The UKC is the first dog registry to offer DNA profiling, an affordable service used for verifying parentage and identifying individual dogs. Results appear on the registration certificate and pedigree. DNA profiling is also used to identify an individual puppy's sire when a bitch has been bred to more than one male, either accidentally or purposefully. It can locate the source of genetic defects, allowing breeders to preserve the integrity of their programs.

What Is a Pedigree?

A pedigree is a chart depicting a dog's ancestors. It lists individual dog names, coat colors, and production records.

Contract

When buying an APBT from a reputable source, you will enter into a contract as part of your sales documentation. This contract contains predictable information, such as the name and address of the kennel, name and address of the purchasers, and statistics on the puppy involved, including birth date, sex, color, parents' names, sale price, and veterinary history. There should also be a guarantee that the puppy is free of genetic faults and can be returned for a refund within a specified time frame. Most breeders include a stipulation that if, for any reason during the dog's lifetime, the buyers decide that they can no longer live with the dog, he will be returned to the breeder, who will find him another home. This important clause eliminates any chance of the dog ending up in a shelter or suffering from inappropriate care. The purchasers don't have to worry about finding another loving home, and the breeder is assured that a dog from one of her litters will never be homeless.

Feeding Instructions

Paperwork from the breeder will include detailed information on what kind of solid food the puppy has been eating, how much of it, and when. This takes the guesswork out of feeding a new puppy and may acquaint you with healthful additives like flaxseed oil. It is a good idea to continue feeding your APBT the same kind of food he's been eating since he was weaned, even if you plan to change it eventually. A puppy's immature digestive system cannot handle abrupt changes in diet, so if you feel strongly about feeding him something else, gradually introduce it into his diet. Start by mixing in one part new food to three parts familiar food for a few days. If he tolerates the change, gradually increase the amount of new food, and decrease the amount of familiar food.

Puppies need to chew, and your breeder will be happy to suggest which chew toys are safe for your APBT. Smaller-size Nylabones are perfect chew toys, as they exercise the puppy's gums and teeth but don't splinter or break.

GENERAL HOME PREPARATION

Before you bring home your new puppy, you will want to make sure his environment is as safe and hospitable as possible. Even though the puppy will not be left unsupervised and uncrated, household hazards must be removed. Your puppy will teethe on anything he can find, and you don't want him latching onto a nice, chewy electric cord or a challenging-but-intriguing cleaning spray bottle.

Perform a walk-through of every area your APBT will be allowed to access—house, garage, and yard—paying attention to anything that might harm him. Potential dangers sometimes lurk in the most unlikely places and in the most unlikely things. These include:

- toxic house- and yard plants
- second-story railings that are spaced widely enough to catch a puppy's head or allow him to fall through
- unsupervised garage access where a puppy can get into toxic fluids, sharp tools, or even be found unexpectedly under the tires of the family car
- heavy objects on shelves that a curious puppy can pull off or topple, causing him to be injured or crushed
- swimming pools, hot tubs, wading pools, and even koi ponds
- small, everyday items like tacks, matches, keys, pens and

How to Register Your APBT

If you are breeding a litter of APBTs, and the sire and dam are both UKC registered, the litter may also be registered. (Remember, the AKC does not register the breed.)

Single-dog registrations are a bit trickier than entire litters. The UKC normally authorizes single registrations only with the consent and cooperation of the regional breed club.

pencils, and razors
• poisonous foods like chocolate and alcohol
• pesticides and cleaners recently applied in and around the house that can make a young dog very sick
• steep stairs and furniture that could cause falls

To prevent serious injury or even death, make your home a safe and happy place for the newest family addition.

City Living

Urban dwellers have pet hazards different from those of their suburban counterparts, especially if they live in an apartment or condominium building. The following are some items to remember if you're bringing an APBT to the big city.

Elevators

Elevators are everywhere in the city: residential buildings, stores, and commercial buildings. When riding with your APBT in an elevator, allow the dog to enter first, in front of you. Follow him quickly inside. Imagining the gruesome scenario of the elevator doors closing with you inside and your dog outside, separated by the leash, is enough to make you conscientious about this tip.

Because puppies need to chew, provide safe chew toys for your dog.

Avoid really crowded elevators when possible,

in addition to elevators that already have an animal rider. The combination of excitement and confined space can lead to trouble.

Escalators

This one is easy. *Never* take your leashed dog on an escalator. The collapsing steps can easily catch a paw, severing toes and causing other injuries.

Rooftops

City folks who don't have the wide open spaces of the suburbs often consider a rooftop as a good place to let their dog run about freely and get some quality exercise. What they may not realize is that dogs have limited distance and depth perception, making the roof a dangerous place. Look for a park on *terra firma* where your APBT can have a good run. It doesn't have to be a dog park; in fact, it shouldn't be a dog park. APBTs are too dog aggressive. Take him for a jog on a leash instead. It's a good exercise plan for both of you.

Windows

If you own a dog, make sure your home windows all have barriers. In many cities, window barriers are mandatory for the safety of residential children, so your building may likely have them already. If not, however, take the initiative to have them installed. Your dog deserves the same kind of safety that a child does.

Common Household Hazards

Keep your APBT away from the following:
- antifreeze
- chocolate
- cleaners and chemicals
- electric cords
- medications and vitamins
- pesticides
- poultry bones
- sharp objects
- toiletries
- toxic houseplants

SUPPLIES

Advance planning will make your APBT's adjustment easier for both of you, so you'll want to purchase a few essentials before you welcome him home.

Food and Water Dishes

The most obvious items to have ready are food and water dishes. They are commonly made of plastic, stainless steel, or ceramic. If you purchase bowls made from any exotic material, ask your vet if it is anything that might cause adverse reactions to the ingredients in your puppy's food, which can make him sick. Even the plastic in feeding bowls can cause an allergic skin

Your APBT's leash should be made of a strong, flexible fabric like nylon or leather.

reaction. Ceramics will shatter or break if dropped, so stainless steel is your best bet.

Collar and Leash

Other must-haves include an appropriately sized collar and leash. The best kind of collar for an APBT puppy is an adjustable nylon buckle collar. It should be small enough to fit his young neck, even if this means you have to upgrade to a larger-size collar when he is fully grown. It should not exert any pressure on his neck. Avoid chain and prong choke collars; their loose fit can catch on things and potentially injure the puppy.

Your APBT's leash should be about 5 (1.5 m) to 6 feet (1.8 m) long and made of a strong, flexible fabric like nylon or leather. Forget retractable leashes; a powerful APBT can break them with his enthusiasm alone. When he is ready to start obedience training, you can use a nylon training collar if you wish, but only at lesson time. These thin training collars that slip over the dog's head do not have attachments for ID tags. A flat buckle collar is better for everyday use.

Grooming Supplies

The short, sleek coat of a healthy APBT requires minimal care to keep it looking beautiful. Unlike longhaired, cold-climate breeds, your APBT's fur needs only a soft brush or grooming glove to remove loose hairs and dander. Later on you may want a shedding comb for those twice-yearly coat sheddings.

Other supplies you will need include a sturdy pair of toenail clippers, a mild, pH-balanced dog shampoo (detergent-based shampoos for humans are too harsh), and a soft toothbrush or finger sheath for dental care. Cotton balls for ear and eye cleaning are probably already in your medicine chest.

Baby Gates

When you need to confine your APBT puppy to a specific area, your best friend can be the baby gate. This will afford your puppy some freedom but keep him from wandering off into unsupervised territory. Gating off stairways is a good idea while your puppy is small, to prevent him from tumbling down a flight and hurting himself.

Keep in mind that baby gates are not infallible. A curious, fearless APBT puppy can figure out that the lattice design or nylon weave of most baby gates makes great climbing walls that are easily scaled. But he can also get his head caught in the lattice or tumble off the top of the gate, so don't count on using it as an alternative to crating while you're away from home.

Provide your dog with age-appropriate toys that are fun and safe.

Toys

The array of available dog toys can be overwhelming. The key is to provide your APBT with age-appropriate toys that are fun *and* safe. Rubbery squeaky toys are a favorite with puppies, as long as you take care that the rubber or plastic isn't readily torn. You don't want your puppy to swallow pieces of the torn toy, or even worse, the squeaker itself. Similarly, stuffed toys provide

hours of shredding fun, but mind that your dog doesn't eat the stuffing. Never give your APBT a stuffed toy that has buttons or any other kind of small appliquéd decorations; they are too easily bitten off and swallowed.

An APBT needs to chew throughout his lifetime. Proper chew

A crate ensures your puppy's safety and is a great housetraining tool.

toys keep him busy and help maintain good oral health. Make sure they are sturdy enough to stand up to the APBT's enthusiastic chewing, but not so hard or brittle that they can injure the dog's mouth and teeth or be swallowed and cause internal injury.

Crate

Select a warm place for the crate where your puppy will rest, away from foot traffic, but where he can still see the family. Young puppies will nap frequently and need a safe, cozy snoozing spot.

Dogs are denning animals who feel secure in a protected or sheltered area. An appropriately sized dog crate will provide this safe haven for your dog and give you peace of mind. With only a brief adjustment period, a properly trained dog will enjoy having "a room of his own" and will often spend quiet time there.

When a puppy must be left unsupervised for any length of time, crating is essential. Not only does this ensure his safety, but it's a great housetraining tool. A puppy instinctively does not want to soil his bed and will soon learn to relieve himself in another designated area. A young puppy's bladder control is minimal, though, so accidents will happen. Line the floor of the crate with thicknesses of black-and-white newspaper that you can easily change when your dog soils them. Some dog owners think the crate is no longer necessary once a puppy is housetrained. On the contrary, an adult APBT who is home alone, uncrated, can find all sorts of mischief—and potential danger—as an outlet for his energy and intelligence.

With the right crate training, a puppy will grow into an adult dog who is comfortable with and secure in his own "den," assuring you of his safety in your absence. But don't think you can buck the system with an oversized crate that the dog can grow into. If you start a small puppy out in a much larger crate, he will discover that he can soil one part of it without compromising his sleeping area. As he grows, increase the size of the crate so that he always has enough room to sit and stand comfortably and turn around. Yes, it costs more to upgrade crate size, but other people are in the same boat. You can often find used crates in perfectly good condition for bargain prices at garage and yard sales.

Supply List

- food and water dishes
- collar and leash
- grooming supplies
- baby gate
- toys
- identification

Identification

The bottom line is that you never want to risk losing your APBT permanently because he cannot be identified. Fortunately, multiple simple, painless ways are available to improve a lost dog's chances for identification and recovery.

Tags

You've already checked to make sure your area has no anti-breed legislation that will impact your APBT. Now you must find out what kind of registration is required, if any. Dog licensing varies from state to state and county to county, so check with your local government. If your dog is issued a tag with an identification number, attach it to his everyday collar. Never give animal control officials a reason to apprehend your APBT.

Equally important is the tag issued by your veterinarian certifying that your dog has been vaccinated against rabies. In the unlikely event that your APBT bites someone, you will need ready proof of immunization. Without it, officials can order your dog to be destroyed to test for possible rabies.

Microchipping

Microchip identification is actually a tiny capsule about the size of a long grain of rice that is injected under a flap of skin on

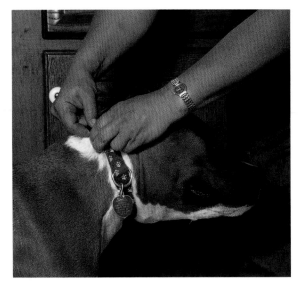

Make sure that your dog's tags are securely fastened to his collar.

the back of a dog's neck. Inside the capsule is a tinier chip with a number that has been registered with an international registry. If a lost dog is turned into an animal shelter or veterinarian, he will be checked for microchip identification with a special scanner. The numbers are read and called into the registry, where they are matched to the rightful owner's contact information.

Microchipping is painless, permanent, and can never be altered, which makes it an extremely reliable method of identification. The chip itself is made of hypoallergenic material and is completely safe for your APBT.

Tattooing

Developed by the founders of the National Dog Registry, tattooing is a simple, affordable means of permanently identifying your APBT. Unlike tattooing of humans, pet tattooing is painless. A dog's skin structure is so different from a human's that the tattoo marker doesn't need to be inserted very deeply into the dog's epidermis, or outer skin layer. Although he may dislike the noise of the equipment and balk at being held still on his side for the procedure, he will feel no pain. Any momentary unpleasantness he experiences is far outweighed by the security a registered tattoo brings.

If there is a downside to tattooing, it is that the tattoo itself may be hard to spot. The best location for a tattoo is on the inside of the thigh, where the hair is sparse and the numbers are readily seen. Check your APBT's tattoo periodically for legibility. The ink will fade over time, but touch ups are free of charge.

A dog who is stolen or lost and subsequently sold to a research laboratory will be returned to its rightful owner, because no research facility will accept any animal with an identifying microchip or tattoo.

SETTLING IN WITH YOUR NEW APBT

Adding an APBT to your household means that, temporarily, your world will revolve around this little guy. After all, living in your home is a big adjustment for him. He will be getting to know not only his new humans, but perhaps some animal family members as well. You will be adjusting, too, because your regular routine will be a little different. Your sleep may even be disrupted for a few nights. However, with a little preparation and the knowledge that the adjustment phase is temporary, you and your new APBT can settle in beautifully together.

Did You Know?

With diligent training, APBTs can live harmoniously with other APBTs and breeds.

The First Nights

Unquestionably, the most difficult time for a puppy and his new family is bedtime. The heart-wrenching cries of a puppy unaccustomed to sleeping alone will sorely tempt you to take him out of his crate and comfort him, but you know the repercussions. He will learn that crying and whimpering not only gets your attention but also gets him into the security of your arms.

To minimize nighttime stress, first make sure that your puppy's crate is warm and cozy. Place it in your bedroom, right next to your bed. He'll feel more secure with you close by. You can put your t-shirt or other piece of worn clothing into the crate; your scent will soothe him. Make a final potty trip with him, kiss him goodnight, and gently put him in his crate and close the door. If he cries, tell him, "No!" firmly. He'll soon learn that crying doesn't get him the coddling he wants.

Having the crate nearby will also expedite housetraining by alerting you to when your puppy wakes up during the night. Take him outside to potty, praise him, and return him immediately to his crate to avoid overstimulation. He should learn that nighttime is for sleeping, not playing.

Multiple-Pet Households

Because APBTs are inclined to be dog-aggressive, introducing one into a multi-pet home requires special care. With diligent training, APBTs can live harmoniously with other APBTs and breeds. If at all possible, though, the new APBT should be of the opposite sex, because aggression and dominance issues can arise between dogs of the same sex.

Two dogs should meet on neutral turf to avoid territorial behavior. Both should be leashed but permitted to sniff and circle each other in the timeless canine dance of greeting. Most adult dogs are kind to and tolerant of puppies, but keep a close eye on them in case of resentment toward the new dog. Do not leave a new puppy alone with an established family dog until you are certain of their compatibility. Even then, an adult dog can accidentally hurt a puppy during rough play. As the dogs get older, the natural "pecking order" will emerge, but occasionally unresolved conflict will remain for the dominant position.

Handle puppy–cat introductions tactfully. Cats usually resent the intruder, often keeping their distance for a few weeks until reconciled with the new addition. When introducing them for the first time, defer to the cat's rank by holding the puppy, not the cat.

Small pets, such as rodents, must be kept away from their natural predators, dogs and cats.

TRAVEL

There will certainly be times when your APBT needs to travel, starting with his trip home with you. Reputable APBT breeders are not as ubiquitous as, say, Labrador Retriever breeders; it's very possible that your new APBT puppy will need to fly to his new home with you. Some boating enthusiasts wouldn't think of spending a day on the water without the family dog, which presents different safety concerns.

Whether by air or by car, traveling with your APBT can be a breeze if you follow a few common-sense rules.

Car Travel

Your APBT's safety and security in the car are as important as any passenger's. You wouldn't think of getting in the car without buckling your seat belt, would you? Your APBT needs the same restraint. In addition to obvious safety benefits in the event of an accident, restraints prevent the dog from suddenly jumping up or otherwise causing you to lose control of your vehicle. Many fine-quality dog harnesses on the market will give your APBT a comfortable and safe ride.

If you opt to keep your APBT crated while traveling by car, ensure that the crate is firmly strapped in place. In some areas, it is illegal to allow your dog to ride unrestrained in the back of a truck. In any case, it is very risky. An abrupt stop can send the dog tumbling around or out of the truck bed. The dog may jump out of the vehicle if he sees something appealing, even if the truck is moving. And let's not even talk about what would happen in a collision.

If a car ride was the first strange thing that separated a puppy from his mother and littermates, he may fear future trips, especially if they take him to the veterinarian. Show the puppy that the car is a good place by lifting him into the car and giving him a treat. Take him out when he finishes. A week or two of this should cure any car fears.

There are two important car-ride caveats. First, don't let your APBT hold his head out of the window of a moving car. Debris can fly into his eyes or ears and cause serious injury. Also, don't leave a dog in a parked car, even with the windows open. A car heats up like a greenhouse and can rapidly cause heatstroke. Open car windows do not provide enough ventilation to

When a Baby Joins the Family

It's easy to let the family dog slip through the cracks when a new baby comes home, but make a concerted effort to reassure your APBT that you aren't forsaking him. (This is important, because dogs often see babies as interlopers into their territory, competing for your love and attention.) Introduce the new baby to your dog before she's even home from the hospital by having your APBT sniff a blanket or shirt with the baby's scent on it. When the baby does come home, allow the dog to sniff the baby. Be sure to pay as much attention to the dog as you do to the baby, and even more when company comes over. Jealousy is not conducive to building a happy, respectful relationship with this new "sibling." You should also give your dog a few extra treats and toys. Before long, your dog will think you brought the baby home just for him!

compensate for hot temperatures. Even on a day when the temperature is mild and pleasant, the car interior can heat up to a dangerous level. If you don't want your APBT to suffer a miserable death, don't leave him in the car.

Air Travel

Air travel can be stressful for dogs. The pressure changes of flight and loud noises on a plane are frightening for novice flyers. Historically, vets prescribed sedatives for dogs scheduled to fly, but the practice has been recently questioned. Some experts think that the decreased heart and respiration rates caused by sedation are more dangerous than the emotional stresses of flying.

Airlines now have strict regulations for animal carriage on commercial flights. Safe air travel is affected by climate and season, both at origination and destination. Dogs must travel in their crates in the cargo compartments of airplanes, unless they are small enough to fit underneath a seat in the passenger cabin. Only very young APBT puppies fit into that category. If you plan to fly your APBT, thoroughly research the airlines' policies on dog transport, documentation requirements, and quarantine laws, if applicable.

To keep your APBT safe in the car, make sure he is restrained at all times.

Foreign Travel

Dogs in military families become seasoned travelers, frequently traveling overseas. However, other cultures do not always hold the same regard as we do for our dogs. Their laws and restrictions can be very different. Quarantine laws vary from country to country, and even within a country. Dogs moving to Hawaii from another American state, for example, must fulfill a quarantine that can last up to 120 days. (Hawaii is rabies free and wants to keep it that way.)

When planning your overseas travel, contact the local consulate for quarantine regulations and health certification requirements. Investigate the airlines' regulations on pet carriage and consider the length and nature of the itinerary. Will a change of plane or airline be required? How long will your dog's confinement last? How will he handle it? Take the same care for your APBT's safety and comfort as you would with any family member.

When You Can't Be There

One of the most important considerations of dog ownership is who will take care of your dog when you cannot.

If you are going to be traveling by air with your APBT, research the airlines' policies in advance.

Doggy Daycare

The first issue to address is your family's lifestyle. Do both adults work full time? If so, a doggie daycare center may be necessary. Many animal shelters will not allow a two-job family to adopt a dog without a daycare plan in place. This isn't indulgence, but responsibility. The emotional well-being of your pack-oriented dog depends on it. An organized daycare program not only prevents separation anxiety and boredom, but it provides great socialization.

With the APBT, however, a daycare facility may not be ideal. Unless very well trained, an APBT's dog-aggressive inclinations make him a questionable candidate for a multi-dog daycare group. A conscientious facility will require you to go through a comprehensive application process and a trial day with your dog at the center to see how he adjusts to the situation. It is gratifying to note that the propaganda surrounding the APBT has not prompted doggie daycare facilities to exclude them or similar breeds.

In-Home Pet Sitting

Once considered a job fit only for the neighborhood kids, professional pet sitters are cropping up every day, to the delight of dog owners who want their APBTs cared for in their own homes. Pet sitters typically visit your dog several times a day to feed and exercise him, as well as administer any medications. Even better is the sitter who will live at your home during your absence. Your dog will enjoy the companionship, and you will be assured of his safety in the event of a health or household emergency.

Traveling Tips

The following are some travel tips to help make your journeys as simple and painless as possible:

- Research dog-friendly lodging in advance.
- If traveling by car, properly secure the dog's crate in the vehicle, or use a seat harness designed for medium-sized dogs.
- If flying, check on airline restrictions regarding animal transportation. Origin and destination climates play an important part.
- If traveling abroad, check on quarantine regulations.
- Ensure that your dog's medical records and inoculations are up to date. Carry a copy of his health certificate with you.
- Never let your dog stick his head out of a moving car window. At best, debris can fly into his eye; at worst, another vehicle could injure or kill him.

Before you allow anyone access to your dog and your home, find out if the sitter is fully bonded and insured. Ask for references. Get a referral from another dog owner, if you can. Invite the sitter to come over and meet your pet while you are present. How does she interact with the dog? Is she experienced with APBTs? Does she have a backup in the event that she is unable to get to your dog? Both you and your dog should feel comfortable being with this person, and vice versa.

Boarding Kennels

A good boarding kennel can be a perfectly acceptable situation for your APBT in your absence. Many dogs enjoy the camaraderie of other boarders and the attention of friendly caregivers. Boarding kennels vary from basic indoor/outdoor cement runs to plush puppy palaces, complete with spa treatments. You may want to stay there yourself!

Before you leave your APBT anywhere for the first time, pay a visit to the facility with your dog. Are the boarding and exercise areas clean and comfortable? Is water always accessible? How much personal, individual attention will your dog receive? Is someone on the premises 24/7?

Not surprisingly, as an APBT owner, you should take your research a step farther. Does the facility have experience with the breed? Do they group dogs together at playtime? Unless your APBT is extremely well trained, you may need to opt out of playgroups to eliminate the possibility of aggression.

Well-socialized APBTs look forward to traveling with their families. Their natural curiosity and enthusiasm turn trips into adventures, whether they occur around the corner or across the state. Planning for their safety and comfort will enhance their experience and give you peace of mind.

YOUR APBT AND THE LAW

Pet population in general has grown to the point that many states, cities, and municipalities have enacted legislation that regulates care of the pet and even how the pet is permitted to interact with society. For APBTs, this has huge implications. Before you add an APBT to your family, thoroughly research what laws in your area may affect you.

Breed-Specific Legislation

Laws against certain breeds deemed "vicious" are in effect in many parts of the country, prohibiting ownership of the applicable breeds. This type of misapplied legislation impacts not only APBTs but often any "bully" breed descended from the ancient fighting dogs, including the American Staffordshire Terrier, the Staffordshire Bull Terrier, the Bull Terrier, and any dog bearing the same characteristics as these breeds. If you live with an APBT in one of these areas, be aware that your dog can be legally confiscated and destroyed, even if he's done nothing controversial (fighting with another dog, growling at a human, jumping on a human). Before you get an APBT or move with one to a new location, check into these laws. It will save you possible heartbreak later on.

Professional pet sitters will typically visit your home several times a day to care for your dog.

Leash Laws

Practically every community has a law requiring pet dogs to be leashed in public. This may seem unfair, because of course your APBT is beautifully trained, but it really is for his safety. Having

By keeping your APBT on a leash, you protect him and other people from injury.

control of your dog at all times protects him from running into the path of a moving vehicle. Even a bicycle can have an accident from trying to avoid hitting a loose dog. By keeping him on a leash, you protect not only your dog from injury, but you protect other people as well.

Licensing Laws

While checking into any breed-specific legislation, you should also check into any dog licensing requirements. Many areas require pets to be officially registered. They receive a tag, similar to the dog's rabies vaccination tag, with the county or city name and a registration number. The fee you pay for this license is money well spent, because it essentially provides a registry that will come in handy if your dog is ever lost. Dog registration also helps the local government keep accurate records on the pet population and ensure that the necessary services for animal control are provided.

"No Pet" Policies

Apartment dwellers should be aware that many buildings refuse to allow pets and will stand fast on this policy. But there may be some cases where a compassionate landlord can be persuaded to let you have a dog. The first step is to introduce the dog to the landlord. A well-mannered, clean, likeable dog can be his own best argument for permission to live there. Buildings that do allow pets usually require some kind of deposit against damage to the apartment. Some buildings also allow some types of pets—cats but not dogs or dogs under a certain weight—so be sure to ask for specifics. Above all, never cause the landlady to regret her decision to allow your APBT in the building or provide an opportunity to add to the ill repute of the breed.

Waste Clean-Up Laws

Not everybody adheres faithfully to this law, as evidenced by the random piles out there. But imagine what our sidewalks and streets would look like if this legislation didn't exist. It doesn't take a lot of time or effort to pick up after your ABPT after elimination, and fancy contraptions aren't necessary. A plastic grocery bag will do the trick just as well.

Just as your decision to add an APBT to your family was made after careful consideration, your home preparation should be just as thorough. Put yourself in the puppy's place; he's going off with a strange family to live in a strange place. It's a little scary. You owe it to him to make sure he is safe and comfortable in your home and your community. The soft bed, cozy crate, and fun chew toys you provide will complement the love and companionship he'll receive, reassuring him that he chose the right humans.

FEEDING
Your American Pit Bull Terrier

Domestic dogs depend completely on their owners for food, so it is essential that we give them a balanced diet of good-quality food that meets their nutritional needs. Without proper nutrition, an APBT pup will not grow into the strong, vigorous dog he is destined to be, and his mental development may suffer. Therefore, it benefits you as an APBT owner to become familiar with all dietary options before selecting the one that best suits your dog's requirements.

FOOD BASICS

Good nutrition is necessary to a dog's well-being. It prevents diseases brought about by dietary deficiencies and helps fight off infections by keeping his immune system working at full throttle. Wholesome dog food containing the right amounts of proteins, carbohydrates, fats, vitamins, and minerals will help keep your APBT feeling and looking his best, as will the right amount of water. The more thoroughly you understand canine nutrition, the easier it will be to feed your dog what he needs and enjoys.

Proteins

Protein is important for bone growth, tissue healing, and the daily replacement of body tissues used up every day. All

The right balance of fats in your APBT's diet will keep his skin healthy and coat shiny.

animal tissue has a relatively high level of protein, but because it is not stored in body tissue, your APBT must replenish his protein supply from his food every day of his life. Because dogs are carnivores, most of the digestible protein they need is found in meat. Too much indigestible vegetable protein can cause colic or diarrhea.

Proteins are made up of about 25 "building blocks" called *amino acids*. Ten of these are *essential*, meaning they cannot be made in the body and must be obtained from food. The other 15 are *nonessential*, meaning that they are made within the body from other amino acids.

Fats

Fat is used as an energy source and keeps your APBT's skin healthy and coat shiny. Finding the right balance of fats is important. A diet too rich in fat results in an overweight dog, leading to other health problems. Too little fat can cause itchy skin, a dull coat, dandruff, and sometimes ear infections. A fat deficiency also fails to protect your APBT from temperature changes, resulting in a dog who is overly sensitive to cold.

The very active and athletic APBT relies on fat as a ready energy source. It also makes his food tasty, thereby encouraging good eating habits.

Carbohydrates

Carbohydrates are comprised of sugars, starch, and cellulose, with simple sugars being the easiest to digest. A dog's carnivorous diet typically does not derive enough carbohydrates from the meat he eats, which is why plant-based carbohydrates are an important component of a balanced diet. Good sources are boiled potatoes, carrots, rice, and whole grains.

Carbohydrates aid digestion and elimination, much the same way high-fiber diets help humans. Approximately five percent of an APBT's complete diet should be fiber from carbohydrates. Excess carbohydrates are stored in the body for future use, but it is difficult to imagine an active APBT with much of an excess.

Vitamins

Vitamins are organic compounds that perform as metabolic regulators in the body. They cannot be manufactured by the body and must be obtained through diet or supplements. Vitamin deficiencies can lead to a variety of health problems, so it is important to receive the full complement of vitamins on a daily basis. A balanced diet should provide all the vitamins your APBT needs. Don't give him vitamin supplements without your vet's okay. It is easy to overdose supplements and create health problems.

Vitamin A

Vitamin A is used for fat absorption in a dog's body, keeping his coat glossy and healthy. It also promotes good eyesight, as well as a normal growth rate and reproduction.

Vitamin B

B vitamins are important for coat, skin, appetite, growth, and eyes. They also protect the nervous system and aid metabolism.

Vitamin C

Vitamin C is synthesized in a dog's own liver, so it is not usually listed in commercial dog food analysis.

Vitamin D

Vitamin D is essential for healthy bones, teeth, and good muscle tone, but it must be taken with the proper ratio of calcium and phosphorus.

Did You Know?

A balanced diet should provide all the vitamins your APBT needs.

Minerals help the body function properly and remain strong.

Vitamin E

Vitamin E is necessary for proper muscle function, the internal and reproductive organs, and all cell-membrane function.

Vitamin K

Vitamin K is synthesized in the digestive tract, so like vitamin C, it is not usually listed in commercial dog food analysis.

Minerals

Minerals are nutrients needed in small amounts by the body to help it function properly and stay strong. They are obtained from food but can also be taken in supplements, where they are often combined with vitamins.

The following minerals are some of the most common:

- **Calcium and phosphorus:** In the correct ratio, calcium and phosphorous work together to prevent rickets and other bone deformities. They also aid in tooth formation, muscle development, and lactation in nursing bitches.
- **Potassium:** Contributes to normal growth and healthy

nerves and muscles.

- **Sodium and chlorine:** Help maintain appetite and normal activity level.
- **Magnesium:** Helps synthesize proteins, as well as prevent convulsions and nervous system problems.
- **Iron:** Needed for healthy blood, aided by copper.
- **Iodine:** Prevents goiter (enlarged thyroid).
- **Zinc:** Promotes healthy skin.
- **Cobalt:** Aids normal growth and keeps the reproductive tract sound, aided by manganese.

As with vitamins, supplement minerals only on your veterinarian's advice.

Water

When you consider that the average dog's body consists of about two-thirds water, it is no surprise that water is necessary for survival. Although dogs don't perspire the same way as humans do, they do lose water through sweat glands in their feet, by panting, and via the kidneys. As a guideline, a healthy dog should take in (from food and drink) 1/2 (14.8 ml) to 3/4 fluid ounces (22.2 ml) per pound (0.45 kg) of body weight per

Make sure that your APBT always has clean, cool water available.

day. Of course, in hot weather or after strenuous exercise, he will drink more.

Make sure that your APBT always has clean, cool water available. If you notice him drinking excessively, talk to your veterinarian. Excessive thirst can be a symptom of illness.

THE DO'S AND DONT'S OF FEEDING

The food that is best for your dog is not always the cheapest, handiest, or most convenient. But because you are committed to giving your APBT the best care possible, you must make the effort to find the right formula for his balanced diet.

Let's start with the basics:

- DO see that your dog's food is tasty for him, or he won't eat it!
- DO read nutrition labels of commercial dog foods, and choose a good-quality, nutrient-balanced food. Avoid foods with chemical preservatives like BHT and ethoxyquin, which are suspected carcinogens. Look for natural preservatives like vitamin E or food without preservatives at all. Consult labels of preservative-free foods for proper storage.
- DO be consistent with the kind of food you choose, as long as it is satisfactory. A sudden change in diet can upset your dog's digestive system, so refrain from jumping from brand to brand.
- DO ensure that fresh, clean, cool water is available at all times.
- DON'T overfeed. Your breeder and/or veterinarian can advise you on the proper amounts and frequency of meals. Don't count on your APBT to stop eating when he's full!

- DON'T feed table scraps. Dogs' bodies are not constructed like ours and therefore do not have the same nutritional needs or food processing capabilities that we do. Some common people foods, such as chocolate and onions, are toxic to dogs. Meat bones other than cooked beef knucklebones can splinter and cause serious injury to your dog's digestive tract.
- DON'T overdo doggy treats. They should supplement your dog's diet, not replace it.

Types of Feeding Bowls

Choosing a feeding dish is a matter of preference, but the pros and cons of each should be considered:

- **Plastic:** Inexpensive but can become scratched and chewed. Difficult to clean properly and can harbor bacteria. Some dogs may develop a skin allergy to the plastic.
- **Stainless steel:** More sanitary than plastic, but so lightweight it is easily knocked over.
- **Ceramic:** Glazed, earthenware bowls are both stable and sanitary, but they are more easily chipped or broken than plastic or stainless steel bowls.

READING THE LABELS

Health-conscious humans have learned to check the labels of store-bought food for nutritional information, and there is no reason that you shouldn't take the same care with your APBT's food. But how can you be sure you're feeding him the right food? It's all there on the label, provided you know what to look for.

When all is said and done, the proof is in the puppy. If your APBT brims over with good health—shiny coat, bright eyes, good appetite, and high energy level—most likely his diet is just fine.

Life Stage

If the label declares the food "100% nutritionally complete," that means that it is appropriate for all life stages. On the other hand, if the label specifies a certain phase, such as "puppies" or "seniors," the food is especially formulated to meet the nutritional needs of that phase. Many senior dog foods contain added glucosamine and chondroitin, which are beneficial to arthritic joints. Dry puppy kibble may be of a finer texture that is easier on a puppy's immature digestive tract.

Ingredients

Ingredients are listed in descending order by amount. The first few ingredients listed compose the bulk of the food, so you want the high-quality ingredients, like meat and whole grains, to be among them.

If your APBT puppy features a shiny coat, bright eyes, and a good appetite, chances are that his diet is just fine.

Be wary of labels that list "animal by-products" as a primary ingredient. This is a euphemism for the animal parts discarded by slaughterhouses (horns, organ linings, beaks, etc.) that are cheap and easy fillers for commercial dog foods. Though not necessarily harmful to your APBT, their nutritional value is dubious.

Guaranteed Analysis

Look on the label for a *guaranteed analysis* chart. This breaks down the levels of protein, fat, fiber, and moisture in the food. This information is nice to know, but it doesn't say much about the quality of the food. The nutritional value of the ingredients is what really matters, not the moisture content.

TYPES OF FOOD

When it comes to nourishing your APBT, the choices these days extend far beyond which brand of horse meat to buy. (Yes, once upon a time, canned horse meat was a popular commercial dog food choice.) Fortunately, dog food companies have made strides in improving the quality of their products, and we are better equipped today to make educated decisions about a healthy canine diet.

Commercial Dog Foods

Commercial dog food is still the most popular way to feed your dog, and dozens of products are available to prove it. In relatively recent years, dog food companies have recognized the special dietary needs of different life stages. Foods are now formulated especially for puppies, healthy adult dogs, overweight dogs, and senior citizens. Formulas also are available that are acceptable for all stages of life, labeled as "100 percent nutritionally complete." However, further food choices must be made within this food type.

Whichever type of commercial food you prefer, opt for a well-balanced, high-quality brand that meets your dog's nutritional needs.

Types of Food

- commercial
- home cooked
- raw
- special (prescription food)
- bones
- treats

Dry Food (Kibble)

Dry dog food is a popular and economical commercial food choice. Dry food keeps well without refrigeration and may be bought in bulk quantities. The chewing action of crunchy dry food also helps reduce tartar buildup on your dog's teeth. Again, read package labels carefully. Ingredients are listed in order of predominance, from greatest to least. Choose a brand that uses a wholesome digestible protein as its primary ingredient—that is, one of the first four listed.

Canned Food

A canned, or wet, diet smells and tastes great to a dog, and it has a long shelf life. It can also be costly, and the soft consistency of the food does little for a dog's oral hygiene.

Canned food is easy to find at supermarkets and convenience stores, but you need to consider how much *digestible* protein it really provides. This largely depends on the type of animal tissue used in the food. *Indigestible* protein passes through the system without breaking down into absorbable nutrients, so a diet with insufficient digestible protein is shortchanging your

Dry food helps reduce tartar buildup on your dog's teeth.

dog. In addition, the higher the water content, the lower the nutrients. Canned dog food is about 75 percent water. A larger portion of high-moisture food must be consumed for the dog's nutritional needs to be met. To be sure that your APBT is getting the most from his canned food, buy only brands labeled "100% nutritionally complete."

Semi-Moist Food

Semi-moist foods are those shaped like chops, burgers, or other meaty-looking facsimiles. But don't be fooled—they are usually the least wholesome of all commercial dog foods, filled with artificial colorings, flavors, and scents. Semi-moist foods do not fit the nutritional bill as an exclusive diet, but they can be served as tasty occasional treats.

The Home-Cooked Diet

Some APBT owners prefer to be in complete control of their dogs' nutrition. Properly researched and prepared, a homemade diet is an excellent way to make sure your dog is eating right.

Make no mistake: The home-cooked diet is no simple can opening or pouch tearing. It requires considerable education and experience to ensure that you are feeding your APBT what he needs. Preparation is time consuming and more costly than buying commercially prepared dog food. In fact, the numbers of people who feed only home-cooked food to their dogs have dwindled in the last 20 years due to the improvement in quality commercial foods. If you feel that your APBT will benefit from a homemade diet, become an expert in canine nutrition. The last thing you want is to deprive him unintentionally of the proper nutrients.

The Raw Diet

It is sometimes difficult to remember that the cuddly APBT sprawled on your lap is descended from a wolf who ate a variety of plant matter in addition to prey. Despite thousands of years of domestication, his digestive system has remained pretty much the same. Dogs have very short intestinal tracts and strong stomach acids that are geared toward consuming and digesting raw food.

Artificial bones made of hard, strong material make good chew toys.

Ideally, a raw diet includes bones and organs in addition to meat. Remember, our dogs' wild ancestors consumed the entire prey, not just the flesh. But what about the small bones of animals like chicken? We have always been told that chicken bones are too dangerous to give our dogs. What we weren't told is that *cooked* chicken bones splinter; raw bones crunch into small pieces that clean the teeth and gums. Bones are also a natural source of calcium and phosphorus. If you plan to transition your APBT to a raw diet, consult your vet on the benefits and risks of bones.

Precautions to Consider

You should take a few precautions when feeding a raw diet. Some are no-brainers for fighting bacteria, such as washing your hands after handling raw meat and thawing frozen meat in the refrigerator instead of at room temperature. Don't microwave raw food, even as briefly as 30 seconds, because it will damage the live enzymes and harden the bones. It is also wise to avoid feeding your dog raw pork, which can transmit trichinella, a parasite historically found in undercooked pork.

As with any new diet, introduce it slowly to your APBT. Incorporate it into his current diet in stages, gradually decreasing the proportion of old food and increasing the amount of raw food.

BARF Diets

There are no magic cures for medical ailments, but many dog owners swear by the BARF (Biologically Appropriate Raw Food) diet, claiming the return to evolutionary roots has relieved their pets of allergies and other skin conditions, cleared up gastrointestinal and chronic ear problems, and maintained good oral health

Why a BARF Diet?

BARF diets contain a great deal of nutrients, and they help keep the coat and teeth healthy, as well as bolster the immune system.

The BARF diet is comprised of raw meat complete with bones, ligaments, and organ tissues. Providing your dog with this diet is more work than pouring kibble into your dog's dish, but the payoff may be worthwhile. More and more people are giving their dogs BARF diets and are thrilled with the results. Teeth are kept clean and white, coats are healthier, and the immune system is bolstered.

BARF diets have been common practice in Europe for years, particularly in Germany. Fear of bacteria and parasites initially kept the United States from embracing the routine, but the tide seems to be changing. After all, dog physiology is designed to accommodate raw food. In fact, the fresher the diet, the more nutrients are available. In addition, the chance of contracting parasites from properly handled human-grade meat is lesser than from wild prey.

Does this mean that all diets other than BARF are unhealthy for your dog? Of course not. But if you think a BARF diet can optimize your APBT's health, do some research and consult with your vet.

Special Diets

Sometimes even an otherwise healthy dog will need a special diet due to specific physical conditions. In these instances, your vet may recommend a prescription food that carefully balances the nutrients known to cause problems.

Dogs with sensitive stomachs or with an allergy to certain foods require a customized diet, such as a lamb and rice formula. Treats may need to be limited to specific ingredients. Your vet will tell you the best protocol to follow.

Bones

Dogs love to chew, and bones are the logical choice. In the wild, dogs chewed and ate the bones of their kill right along with the meat, which provided essential minerals and a dental cleaning to boot. Nowadays, it is up to us to provide the right kind of bones to satisfy our dogs' need to chew.

The old adage about the dangers of cooked chicken bones still rings true. Small animal bones splinter easily and can injure a dog's intestinal tract or cause choking. So what kind of bone can your APBT enjoy safely? Large soup bones sold in the meat section of your supermarket are a convenient and popular choice. Dogs love to eat the marrow inside, and the thick bone gives his teeth and gums a good workout. Given enough time, though, APBTs will probably break off small pieces. To avoid choking hazards, toss the bone away when it becomes too brittle.

Artificial bones made of hard, strong material make good chew toys. Some are coated with a tasty meat or peanut butter flavor; others have a soft, nubbly texture designed to massage the dog's gums as he chews. These "bones" are virtually indestructible and provide hours of chewing pleasure without a worry.

Treats

It's as important to know what's in the treats you give your dog as it is to know the ingredients of his primary food. Unwholesome snacks and treats can negate all the health benefits you have worked so hard to achieve.

As with food, dog treats come in a variety of sizes, shapes, and compositions. Some are made with only natural, wholesome ingredients suitable for human consumption; others contain mostly chemicals and animal by-products. Many are available at supermarkets; others are only found at pet specialty stores. The whole and natural foods markets that are springing up everywhere usually have a pet products aisle where you can find nutritious dog treats. They may cost a little more, but the ingredients are top quality.

You may be surprised to know that some of the best dog treats are right in your kitchen. Share some sliced apple or bell pepper with your APBT. Rice cakes make a satisfying, low-calorie snack, and a tablespoonful of natural peanut butter is always a crowd pleaser. Remember, though, that some foods that humans eat can make your dog very sick, so check with your vet before experimenting.

Supplements

A wholesome diet should provide all the nutrients your APBT needs, but at some times in a dog's life, food supplementation is beneficial. For example, a pregnant or nursing female needs a little more food than she normally does. Show dogs who are frequently on the road may experience more stress than "civilian" dogs, and they may need more nutrition. If you feel your APBT would benefit from extra food or nutritional supplements, consult your vet first. Supplements are easily overdosed, which can lead to a variety of ailments.

FEEDING FOR EVERY LIFE STAGE

You wouldn't feed pepperoni pizza to an infant or peanut brittle to a senior citizen with dental problems. Your APBT's life stages should also be taken into consideration when planning his meals. The food you give your puppy has a different nutritional make-up than an adult dog's maintenance diet, and a geriatric dog with a slower metabolism will benefit from a diet lower in fat and calories. Just as each dog is an individual, your APBT's food shouldn't be one size fits all. Your breeder or vet can guide you in adapting to your dog's changing dietary needs.

Feeding Your APBT Puppy

All things being equal, the nutritional needs of an APBT puppy are no different from those of any other breed. Puppies need fresh, frequent, small meals of a good-quality food, and they need fresh water to be accessible at all times.

Your puppy will have been weaned about four to six weeks before you take him home, so find out what his breeder has been feeding the litter, and stock up on the same kind of food. Even if you ultimately want to feed him a different brand or type of food, you will need to make the change gradually by mixing it with the food he is used to. A puppy's immature stomach is not equipped to handle abrupt dietary changes.

As a general rule of thumb, an APBT puppy will eat four times a day until he is about two years old. As he grows, the number of feedings can be reduced to three and then finally to two as he reaches adulthood. Dogs mature at varying rates, so adjust the feeding schedule accordingly. An old school of thought advocates a single meal a day for adult dogs, but a healthier choice is to divide his daily ration into two meals.

In general, APBT puppies will eat four times a day until they are about two years old.

How much is an appropriate amount of food at each meal? Your breeder or vet can guide you on this. Commercial dog food packages usually provide guidelines to feeding, based on the age and weight of your puppy. Puppies can have voracious appetites, but be careful not to overfeed. If your puppy seems insatiable, and your vet approves, add a little bit of cooked rice or whole-grain, low-sugar cereal to his ration of dog food. It won't add a lot of extra calories, and the bulk will keep him satisfied longer.

Treats will certainly be a part of your puppy's diet, especially when you are introducing him to early obedience training and housetraining. You can buy them or make them yourself, but remember that table scraps are never part of a balanced canine diet. When feeding your dog treats, be sure that they are made of wholesome, easily digestible ingredients. Healthy treats supplement a puppy's diet; they don't replace his primary food.

Feeding the Adult APBT

In general, an APBT puppy is considered fully grown after

Sample Feeding Schedule

Use this table as a guideline, not a rule:

Age	Feeding Schedule
Weaning to six months	Four times daily
Six months to one year	Three times daily
One to two years and older	Once or twice daily

the age of two years, although some say that a one year old is close to adulthood. Maturity can arrive sooner for some dogs than for others. A typical adult APBT eats two meals a day; gradually decrease the number of feedings as he grows. This can vary, of course, depending on your dog's individual needs. A neutered adult will require less food than an active show dog, and a game-bred APBT who participates regularly in Schutzhund or hunting will require even more than a show dog. Even dogs with the same lifestyles can have slightly different metabolisms and require more or less food. Some dogs eat more in winter than in summer. Experiment until you find the right amount and frequency of feedings that best suit your dog. His bright eyes, shiny coat, healthy musculature, and happy disposition will tell the tale.

Feeding the Older APBT

As with humans, a dog's metabolism slows down as he ages. Just like his maturation from puppy to adult, the aging rate can vary from dog to dog. Technically, an APBT aged seven and older is considered a senior citizen. As he grows older, your APBT might show less interest in his food for a variety of reasons. One might be dental issues. If your dog has sore teeth, mealtime is no picnic for him, but your vet can suggest how to work around this problem. Or maybe old age has dulled your APBT's senses, making him a picky eater. You might try warming his food to give it a more appetizing aroma or offering the food in smaller amounts several times a day instead of one or two big meals. The change may entice a fussy older dog to eat.

Geriatric dogs thrive on food that has a lower percentage of protein than what they ate during their prime, and "senior formula" dog foods are manufactured with this in mind. They also contain less fat and feature added nutrients like glucosamine and chondroitin for good joint health. Read and compare nutrition labels to find the best food for your older APBT.

FEEDING SCHEDULES

Basically, you can feed your APBT in two ways: free feeding or scheduled feeding. As the name implies, free feeding describes a method in which unlimited food is provided all the time. Scheduled feeding is, well, on a schedule. Common sense tells us that specific amounts of food at particular intervals is the healthy way to feed an APBT, yet some dog food companies advocate free feeding. Which is right for your APBT? To weigh the pros and cons, you first have to understand the options and their repercussions.

Scheduled Feeding

Scheduled feedings help regulate elimination, which in turn aids you in housetraining. If you take your dog outside after every meal, he is sure to go, reinforcing the potty message. An APBT on a feeding schedule is also less susceptible to digestive upsets. He'll be less apt to gulp his food, a bad habit that can lead to gastric torsion, a dangerous and often fatal medical condition.

The only real disadvantage of scheduled feeding is the constraint it puts on your personal freedom. Unlike cats, whose owners can leave with sufficient food and water for days at a

Is Your APBT at the Proper Weight?

Healthy APBTs can range in size from 30 pounds (13.6 kg) to 75 pounds (34.0 kg), with a few standouts at 100 pounds (45.4 kg). The best guideline is the dog's general appearance. Look at pictures of APBTs at different sizes and corresponding weights. Does your dog look like one of those?

Another way to gauge proper weight is to gently run a hand over your dog's rib cage. If the dog is overweight, you won't feel his ribs. If he is underweight, the ribs will show prominently all the time. At a healthy weight, you will be able to feel his ribs with gentle pressure and see them lightly outlined beneath the skin.

A regular feeding schedule can help prevent digestive upsets.

time, dogs need someone there at mealtime to dole out the food. Most dogs will eat as much food as you make available all at once. You can't set out food for two or three meals and expect your APBT to ration it while you are gone for the day. If you can't be there, arrange for someone who can.

To keep the "scheduled" in "scheduled feeding," limit the time that meals are available to your APBT. Even if your dog doesn't eat all of his food right away, pick up the dish after ten minutes. He will quickly learn that he has a certain window of opportunity to eat if he doesn't want to wait until his next scheduled meal.

If you have a lifestyle that keeps you away from home during the day, have someone come in a few times to feed the puppy and take him outside. He'll be on a frequent-meal schedule for several months, and you'll need to accommodate it.

Free Feeding

You know those elaborate midnight buffets served on cruise ships? Imagine having one at home, around the clock, every day of the week. That's what free feeding your APBT amounts to. Most dogs won't stop eating when they no longer feel hungry, and a free-feeding APBT will probably become overweight, lethargic, and passionless about his food, impeding obedience training. After all, would you get excited at the prospect of a treat if you had them staring you in the face all day long?

Dogs in the wild have long interludes between meals; their digestive systems are not designed to accommodate continuous eating in unlimited amounts. They need to rest after digestion and prepare for the next meal.

Free feeding can promote begging, an annoying habit that your APBT doesn't need to learn. If his food is available at all times, he's going to get pretty bored with it. Your hamburger will smell a lot more tempting than the same old kibble in his bowl. Soon he will ignore his food completely and wait for handouts from your dinner table. This is not only bad manners but may deprive him of optimum nutrition, which is the foundation of any good-tempered and happy pet.

The only advantage to free feeding is that it sets *you* free from having to make a trip home to feed the dog. Free feeding doesn't do your dog any good, though. If he doesn't gorge on the food all at once, it will sit out for a long period of time, becoming unappetizing and possibly spoiled.

OBESITY

Healthy adult males typically weigh 35 (15.9 kg) to 75 pounds (34.0 kg); females, 30 (13.6 kg) to 60 pounds (27.2 kg). Dog food packages list recommended servings based on a dog's age and weight. Your dog may require more or less; his behavior and appearance will be your guide.

Even a fit APBT can mask a few extra pounds (kg) behind that naturally stocky build. How can you determine if he is overweight, then? Your veterinarian's scale is one way; another is to run your hands along the dog's sides. If you can readily feel his ribs, and no excess rolls are present around his neck, his weight is satisfactory. An obese dog will have noticeable rolls of fat, especially in a seated position, and you won't be able to feel his ribs without applied pressure.

An overweight APBT is an unhealthy dog, period. Obesity puts added stress on his joints and forces his internal organs to

Canine Obesity Concerns

- Depression
- Diabetes
- Gastrointestinal disorders
- Heart problems and respiratory disease
- Heat intolerance
- Joint and bone problems
- Liver disease
- Skin conditions

Feeding Routine

Dogs love routine. If you feed your dog at approximately the same times every day, it won't take him long to know when that time approaches. You might find him waiting patiently by his feeding station or where the dog food is stored. Their internal clocks help keep their humans on schedule and prevent bad habits like drooling and begging.

work harder. An overweight APBT can also develop diabetes, skin conditions, heat intolerance, and depression.

At some point during the aging process, your APBT's metabolism will slow down. If you don't reduce the amount of calories accordingly, he'll gain unneeded weight. The "food is love" philosophy makes no more sense for your dog than it does for the humans in your family. Saying no to extra treats and junk food snacks isn't harsh. You are demonstrating your love by keeping his weight at a proper level. In addition to monitoring his food intake, regular exercise will help a healthy adult APBT keep that beautiful physique.

TABLE MANNERS

No one likes sitting down to a meal only to have a whining dog at her side, begging for a handout. Or placing her plate of cookies on the coffee table when the phone rings, only to come back and find it licked clean. Teaching your APBT good manners around food is important not only for social reasons but for his own well-being. Food is a powerful incentive for both good behavior and bad, and you want to teach your APBT the right way to conduct himself around food.

Because you do not give your APBT table scraps, begging at the dinner table shouldn't be an issue. But when you can't finish those last few bites of tuna or hamburger and can't bear to throw them out, don't move the plate from the table to the floor and let the dog have the food. Instead, clear it away from the table, and surreptitiously scrape the food into his bowl at his usual feeding spot. That way, your dog won't associate this special treat with your dinner table and consequently learn to beg.

When you decide to give your dog a treat, make it a learning opportunity. Even if he is an obedience champion, have him sit before you give him the treat. This reinforces the rewards of good behavior and dissuades him from jumping on you and snapping the goodie from your fingers.

Assuming that you are giving him a food he likes, your APBT should start eating as soon as you put the bowl down. If he doesn't show immediate interest in his food, he may have an upset stomach. If he doesn't start eating within 20 minutes, remove the food and discard it. Once his stomach settles down, he will gladly eat his next meal. On the other hand, if he is just being finicky, he will learn that there is a certain window of opportunity for food. If he wants to eat, he needs to do so when his meal is served to him.

Although food is an effective training tool, you should never deprive your APBT of food for training purposes. Survival instincts overrule an APBT's desire to please his human, and a hungry dog will do whatever it takes to get food. Aside from the fact that you owe your dog the security and basic health of regular, quality food, you want him to learn the positive rewards of obedience.

Your APBT needs the right food for growth, work, and body maintenance; you committed yourself to providing this basic need when you became a dog owner. If you are doing your job correctly, your APBT will thrive, letting you know by his bright eyes, happy disposition, and shiny coat that you are living up to your end of the bargain.

Don't feed your dog leftovers from the table, or he might learn to beg every time a meal is served.

GROOMING

Your American Pit Bull Terrier

The votes are in—the APBT is one of the handsomest dog breeds around. The bright eyes, sleek coat, and dazzling smile of a healthy APBT cut a stately figure. And it doesn't take a Herculean effort to keep him looking that way. Regular grooming sessions do more than just touch up your dog's gorgeous bod. They are a great way for you and your APBT to spend quality time together. Gentle grooming, especially with a glove, is essentially a kind of petting, turning the grooming session into a loving interaction that is pleasurable for both of you.

GROOMING SUPPLIES

APBTs have a short, smooth coat that puts them among the easiest dog breeds to groom. Unlike Afghan Hound owners, who could open their own beauty salon, you won't need a lot of equipment. APBT coat and skin care is minimal, but you will need to get a few basic grooming supplies from your local pet-supply store. Store them in a handy bin or box that will prevent blades from rusting and keep everything in one place.

Brush

The type of brush most often used for the APBT has a handle and medium-soft bristles to make his coat gleam.

A palm-sized rubber curry brush is useful for times when your APBT has frolicked in something especially messy. The rubber nubs remove serious dirt on the upper body once the coat has dried.

A carder brush brings out dead undercoat hair with its bent wire bristles, but not necessarily better than a bristled brush.

Comb

Combs are available in plastic or metal, although the plastic ones tend to break or be chewed by the dog, perhaps intentionally! Whatever the material, the comb's teeth should be rounded both at the tips and in cross section to prevent tearing hair or skin. Combs are either wide-tooth or fine-tooth. Short APBT hair doesn't require the meticulous combing that a Lhasa Apso or a Silky Terrier does, but a comb can be useful during seasonal shedding times to separate the undercoat and bring up any loose, dead hair.

Nail Clippers

Two types of clippers are available. The guillotine type works well for an APBT puppy, but as dogs grow older, their nails thicken and don't cut as easily. That's when you should switch to the clippers that look and act like shears. If possible, have a professional groomer or veterinary technician demonstrate how each type functions. If you are at ease with the equipment, the nail trimming session will be quick and easy.

Shampoo

The only suitable shampoo for your APBT is one specially formulated for dogs. Even the mildest of baby shampoos designed for humans are too harsh for dogs. At worst, they can cause adverse skin reactions; at best, they strip the dog's skin of natural oils. Skin that is too dry can become itchy, and excessive scratching can lead to uncomfortable conditions requiring medical treatment. With regular brushing, your APBT's short hair will stay clean without shampoos.

Doggy Toothbrush and Toothpaste

To brush your APBT's teeth, use a new human toothbrush or a finger sheath, which is

Choosing a Groomer

The APBT requires so little grooming that it seems unnecessary to use a professional groomer. However, if you decide that this is a good option for you, here are a few things to check out first:

- Are you confident that your APBT will cooperate with a groomer? His training must be impeccable before you can turn him over to the ministrations of someone else.
- How experienced is the dog groomer? An easy-care APBT may be a good first client for an inexperienced groomer, but is a first-time groomer good for an APBT?
- Does the groomer have experience with APBTs? You don't want someone who is fearful of handling your dog.

a textured sleeve that fits over your forefinger and gently rubs away plaque.

What you should *not* use is human toothpaste, for the same reason that small children under the age of five should not use it—neither is able to spit it out. Human toothpaste is not made for consumption by man or beast. Because your APBT will swallow whatever you use to clean his teeth, make sure you give him one of the yummy-flavored dog toothpastes available at pet supply stores.

Grooming Supplies

- brush
- comb
- nail clippers
- shampoo
- doggy toothbrush and toothpaste

COAT CARE

Your APBT's coat does more than give you something to vacuum off the sofa cushions. It protects his skin from the elements and keeps him warm in cold weather. It is also a barometer of his overall health. A healthy APBT will have a shiny, clean-smelling coat. A dull, lackluster coat may indicate a dietary deficiency or some other medical problem. Bare patches where fur has fallen out are a sure sign of trouble, usually mange or another skin ailment.

A beautiful coat is all the well-dressed APBT needs to strut his stuff to the world. With good care from you, it will be comfortable and handsome for the duration of his life.

Examining the Skin

Grooming provides an excellent opportunity to give your APBT the once-over for ticks, fleas, or skin lesions, because his short hair makes irregularities easy to spot. In fact, because the APBT's fur lies flat against his skin, a biting tick disrupts the smooth, even surface of his coat. You might catch the small bump with your eyes, and you can feel it by running your hand gently over his coat.

How to Examine Your APBT's Skin

Check the fur for "hot spots," which are possible irritations that may cause your APBT to scratch, lick, or nip at his skin. Possible skin ailments run the gamut from heat rash to mange mites. If you feel your APBT is having discomfort due to a skin problem, consult your vet. Most skin issues are easily treatable. Dry skin or dandruff can be helped by adding 1 tablespoon (14.8 ml) of canola, safflower, or flax oil to his food. The short-

chain fatty acids in the oil lubricate the skin from the inside out.

Brushing

Brushing an APBT's coat is a snap, thanks to his short, smooth hair. A short, dense-bristled brush with a handle is your best bet for routine brushings.

How to Brush Your APBT

Follow the direction of the hair, starting at the head and working back toward the tail. Apply enough pressure to stimulate the skin but not so much that it causes your dog discomfort. Be particularly gentle when brushing the belly and undersides or if you hit any "ticklish" areas that make his skin twitch.

During molting times, a shedding comb is great for removing dead hair and undergrowth. A shedding comb is a metal loop with a handle that has small, fine teeth on one side and larger, more widely spaced teeth on the other. Be careful not to apply too much pressure when combing, because the teeth can easily dig into the APBT's skin.

Bathing

Unless he rolls around in something mysteriously offensive, your APBT won't need much bathing during his lifetime. Regular grooming with a brush or comb should be enough to maintain a shiny, clean, fresh-smelling coat. Excessive bathing robs the dog's skin of essential oils and can lead to itching or a rash, so bathe only as necessary. If you feel strongly about regular baths, keep the frequency down to once a month, and stay away from bath and shampoo products intended for humans. They contain detergent and are too harsh for a dog's skin. Opt for a mild dog shampoo instead.

Some dogs stoically endure their baths; others need an extra set of arms to keep them from jumping out of the tub and trailing sudsy water in their wake. But some dogs like water and actually enjoy bath time. During warm weather, bathe your APBT outdoors and turn bath time into playtime. Turn on the lawn sprinklers and have your dog romp through the spray before and after he's lathered up. (Of course, too much fun may get him dirty again and you'll have to start over.) Take care to keep the lather to a minimum to keep suds from getting into his eyes. If you prefer a more traditional cleansing, plastic kiddie pools make great outdoor bathtubs. Set the garden hose to a gentle spray for wetting his coat and rinsing off soapsuds, and wipe his paws dry before going inside.

Genuine Versus Synthetic Bristles

Some professional groomers dislike brushes with synthetic bristles, saying they generate too much static electricity. It may be worth buying a genuine bristle brush, if possible.

How to Bathe Your APBT

When an indoor bath is necessary, choose a location with a comfortable temperature, free from drafts. The water temperature also should be comfortably warm. You want to make the bath environment as comfortable and pleasant as possible to encourage your APBT's cooperation. Once the running water is at the right temperature, lift the dog into the tub or shower stall. Barrel-chested breeds like the APBT should be lifted with one arm around the front of his chest and the

Shedding

Daily shedding is not as big a deal for APBTs as it is for longhaired breeds. APBTs don't have the thick undercoat of some breeds like Collies and Keeshonds, thus sparing you a vacuuming nightmare. But they will "blow their coat" twice yearly. In autumn, they will shed their summer coats in favor of thicker ones to prepare for winter. In the spring, that heavier coat will be replaced by lighter fur.

You will know it is shedding season when stroking your dog with a bare hand loosens gobs of hair. A gentle combing with a shedding comb will remove this loose undercoat and distribute natural skin oils. Be cautious of any areas on your APBT's body that are more sensitive than others, such as open or healing wounds and irritations. In addition, some dogs have ticklish areas on their underbelly, where combing or brushing causes an unpleasant sensation.

other arm around the back of his legs, below the rump. Lifting with your arms underneath his chest and stomach can put uncomfortable pressure on his organs.

Give the dog a minute or two to get used to the feel of the water. Gently wet down his coat with a hand-held shower attachment. If you don't have one, use a large plastic cup or bowl to pour the water. Gently soap up his body from the neck down, avoiding his head. Treat him to a gentle body massage as you work the lather, and don't forget his underbelly and legs.

The head and face require special attention, because you don't want to get soapy water inside his ears and eyes. Dampen a clean washcloth with warm water, and gently wipe around the eyes and nose. If soap does accidentally get into his eyes during the bath, ease the sting with a drop or two of mineral oil in the corner of each eye.

Use the washcloth to gently wipe clean his outer ears and a cotton ball dipped in mineral oil to gently clean the inner ear. Never stick anything down inside the ear, because you can damage delicate tissues.

When he's ready for rinsing, set the spray attachment on a soft setting, and take your time getting out all traces of soap. Shampoo residue will leave the coat looking dull and may cause itching. If you don't have a spray nozzle, it's a little more challenging to rinse off the underbelly. Try gently splashing rinse water with a cup. If he's very cooperative, raise the front half of his body with your arm behind his front legs, so that he's standing on his back legs. Keep a firm hold so that he doesn't lose his balance. With your other hand, rinse off the exposed belly.

When your APBT is completely rinsed off and ready to get out of the tub, get ready for your own shower, because the first thing he'll do is shake all the excess moisture from his coat. You're probably already wet from assisting your APBT safely out of the tub, but you may not want the entire room drenched. Have a large towel ready to envelop him and briskly rub his coat until he's barely damp. Take care that he isn't exposed to any cold drafts before he's completely dry.

NAIL TRIMMING

When man domesticated dog, he became obliged to take over

Grooming as Bonding Time

What APBT wouldn't enjoy the loving touch of his human? There is no better way to spend quality time with your APBT than with regular grooming sessions. Brushing his short, smooth coat will remove most dirt and reduce the need for baths. Use a soft bristle brush or currying glove, and his grooming session will feel like a relaxing spa treatment.

certain tasks from Nature. Regular nail trimming is one of them. Dogs in the wild don't have this problem because they cover enough terrain in their daily quest for food to keep toenails worn down to a practical length. If you regularly walk your APBT, his nails may be kept short naturally. Most dogs, however, will need a little help from their humans.

If toenails are allowed to grow too long, they will interfere with the dog's natural walk. He will tend to walk on the back of his feet, which can cause splayed toes and an unappealing gait. With extreme neglect, unclipped toenails will eventually curl under the foot and puncture the toe pads. Long toenails are also at risk of catching on a tree root or other obstacle and causing a painful injury to the toe.

Toenail clippers come in several blade sizes and styles. Choose the right one based on your dog's age and the thickness of his nails. The clippers you buy for your puppy's tiny, soft nails won't suffice for your adult's thicker nails. Ask your breeder or vet for guidance in selecting the right appliance.

How to Trim Your APBT's Nails

Dogs don't like having their feet and toes handled if they aren't used to it, so nail trimming should begin in puppyhood to acclimate your APBT to the practice. Start by gently fingering a young puppy's paws and massaging his toes so that he will learn to accept your touch and even enjoy it.

To clip the toenails, lift the foot up and forward in one hand, using your dominant hand to do the trimming. If your dog's toenails are white, you will be able to see the quick, the blood vessel in the bottom of the nail stem. Trim the nail outside the

Begin nail trimming during puppyhood to acclimate your dog to the practice.

quick. If his nails are black, place a small flashlight directly behind the nail. You will see a darker spot where the blood vessel begins. If you still aren't sure, err on the side of caution. If you trim the nail too short, you will cut the quick.

Proper nail trimming is painless, but accidents happen. A sudden movement of the dog's foot can cause you to accidentally cut the nail quick. If this happens, he'll let you know by yipping and jerking his foot out of your hand. No doubt you'll feel worse about it than he does. Stop the bleeding by using a styptic pencil or styptic powder (found in any drugstore). Home remedies to stop bleeding include applying a little cornstarch or pressing the nail into a soft bar of soap for a minute or two. Your stoic APBT will forgive the rare accidental cut, but if it happens too often, he will probably head for the hills when you open the drawer where the clippers are stored.

When cleaning your APBT's ears, gently wipe away any surface dirt without poking down inside the ear.

EAR CARE

Whether or not your APBT's ears have been cropped, they will need regular attention from you to stay clean and healthy.

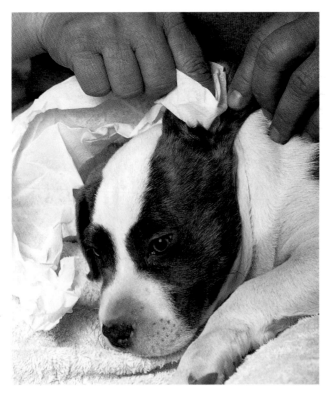

Routine inspection of your dog's ears will enable you to spot parasites like ticks and ear mites or any irritation or discharge present that could indicate infection. Dogs who run through underbrush need to have their ears checked for burrs, cuts, and scratches.

How to Care for Your APBT's Ears

As stated earlier, clean your APBT's ears with a cotton ball dipped in a little mineral oil. Gently wipe away any surface dirt, paying attention to the nooks and crannies as best as you can without poking down inside the ear. Don't attempt to deep-clean any wax buildup yourself;

your vet will check for it during routine exams and recommend treatment.

How do you know if an ear problem exists? Your APBT's behavior will tell you. If he frequently shakes his head, scratches his ear with a foot, or rubs his ear on the floor, look inside. Redness or discharge indicates an inflammation or infection. Yeast infections, which are a common side effect of antibiotic medication, produce an annoying itch and an ill-smelling discharge. An immediate visit to the vet is in order. She will probably prescribe medicated ear drops to ease the discomfort and irritation. To administer drops, hold the earflap gently away from the head and drop the recommended dosage into the ear canal. Replace the flap and gently massage the outside of the ear to work the drops in and minimize loss when he shakes his head.

EYE CARE

No less important in an APBT's health care regimen is ongoing eye care. The easiest and most obvious step to providing that care is to check your home environment for sharp objects at eye level and to examine your dog's eyes frequently for signs of infection or injury.

How to Care for Your APBT's Eyes

First, remove anything inside that poses a potential danger. Outdoors, environmental threats include air pollution, thorny plants, and heavy underbrush. This bully breed runs the special risk of eye damage from human bullies, like children throwing stones at the neighborhood "pit bull." As always, vigilant supervision of your APBT is the best defense against dangers of all types.

Dogs are subjected to many of the same eye conditions as humans, including sties, infections, allergies, and as they get older, cataracts. A healthy dog will normally secrete clear mucus from his eyes that is easily wiped away with a soft, damp washcloth, cotton ball, or commercial "tear stain" wipes favored by dog show participants. If the discharge appears yellowish or bloody, something is wrong, and you must consult your vet right away.

Routine eye exams by you and your vet will minimize any

Ear Cropping

Ear cropping is a subject of much controversy in the dog community. It was a common practice in the days of pit fighting because handlers didn't want the opponent to get an ear hold, as torn or bitten ears would bleed profusely. Moreover, a lack of floppy ears to grab encouraged the fighting dog to go for a throat hold.

Today, no practical reason exists for ear cropping. It does not prevent ear disorders, as is sometimes thought. Some APBT enthusiasts prefer the stern appearance cropped ears give the dog and consider it an important facet of the APBT's handsome appearance, but it is not mandatory. The UKC breed standard for the APBT states that ears may be cropped or not cropped, an option unavailable to AmStaffs and other AKC-recognized breeds in the show ring.

Ear cropping is illegal in most European countries as a result of the 1987 European Convention for the Protection of Pet Animals. One day, the practice may be prohibited in the United States, but for now, American APBT owners have a choice.

If you decide to have your APBT's ears cropped, the vet will do it when the pup is a few months old. The ear is cropped relatively short to create the "prick ears" APBTs are known for. This eliminates the need for the postsurgical training necessary with longer-eared cropped styles, such as those of the Great Dane and the Boxer. The prick ears will stand up on their own as they heal, without splints. Because the cropped APBT look is different from that of other traditionally cropped breeds, a vet experienced with APBT ears should perform the procedure.

problems your dog may have. You want your APBT's eyes to be clear and bright for a lifetime.

ANAL SAC CARE

Nobody will admit it, but at some time or another, everyone has wondered why dogs don't need toilet paper. The answer lies in two glands that produce a substance that helps pass the stool cleanly. The small glands are located on either side of the anus, just under the skin, and open to the outside by tiny ducts or sacs. Wild animals with these sacs also use them for protection (like skunks) or for scent marking of territory, but domestic animals have pretty much lost the ability to empty these sacs voluntarily. Occasionally they clog up, making your dog very uncomfortable and causing a risk of infection.

If impacted anal sacs are not eventually emptied, an abscess can form and possibly rupture out through the skin. The condition is painful, messy, and malodorous. The dog should see a vet right away, who will prescribe antibiotics.

You will know anal gland congestion is present if your APBT begins to scoot along the floor on his haunches, trying to ease the discomfort. You also may notice him licking under his tail.

The foul-smelling, brownish fluid in the sacs needs to be expressed, which your vet can do quickly and easily. Your dog should feel immediate relief, though in extreme cases it may take a couple of consecutive expressions before the sacs stay empty. Added fiber to the diet can help empty the sac by creating a bulkier stool that absorbs more of the fluid as it passes through the dog's system.

How to Empty Your APBT's Anal Sacs

If you want to purge the glands yourself—and this is not for the squeamish—the procedure is uncomplicated. Use one hand to hold his tail up, and with a couple of tissues in your other hand, take the skin on either side of the anus, just below the middle, in your thumb and forefinger. Push in slightly and squeeze gently. The nasty evidence of your success will be on the tissue, and the dog will stop scooting.

Although all dogs have these glands, not all dogs experience problems with them. Your APBT may go through life without anal sac problems at all. But if you notice any of the following symptoms, make an appointment with the vet:

- Reluctance to eat
- Depression or listlessness
- Sudden swelling or drainage near the anus
- Constant licking of the anus
- Vomiting

Anal Sacculectomy

If your APBT's anal sacs need to be emptied every few weeks or more, you may choose to have them surgically removed. This procedure is not without risk, however. Many local nerves control fecal incontinence, and even a change in the local musculature of the sphincter can affect fecal incontinence. You could be trading one problem for another, bigger one.

DENTAL CARE

Public awareness of the benefits of routine canine dental care has risen in the past few decades. People are realizing the importance of good oral health maintenance for their pets as well as for themselves. The further our canine companions have come from their feral origins, the more assistance they need from us to maintain good dental hygiene.

Tooth Brushing

In the wild, a dog's diet consisted of the bones and meat of his prey. Teeth were naturally kept clean of tartar by the chewing action of the bones and tendons. Now that domesticated dogs mostly eat a commercial diet with little natural abrasion, it is up to us to see to their oral hygiene.

How to Brush Your APBT's Teeth

Begin routine oral care when your APBT is a puppy. He should learn to willingly accept your fingers or a toothbrush in his mouth so that, as a strong adult, he will be cooperative. Your regular grooming sessions are a good time to inspect his mouth for any signs of dental trouble.

To brush your APBT's teeth, first acquaint him with the process. Don't even use a toothbrush the first few sessions; just gently stroke the outside of your APBT's cheeks with your finger. Once he's comfortable with that, put a dab of doggy toothpaste on your finger for him to taste. At this point, you can move on to the actual toothbrush, or cover your finger with a dental sheath before applying the toothpaste to it. Start by brushing just a few teeth, gradually increasing to all of them. Be sure to get the rear molars, where plaque has a greater tendency to accumulate. Work up to about 30 seconds per side. Dogs don't get much tartar on the inside surfaces of their teeth, so you only need to brush the outer surfaces. When you finish, lavish praise on your APBT, and he will learn to look forward to tooth brushing.

Keeping your APBT's mouth clean is easier than ever thanks to the many canine dental hygiene products created with the dog's taste buds in mind. Toothpastes are available that taste like chicken and beef, as are flavored finger sheaths you rub on teeth and gently massage gums with, and flavored, textured chew toys that scrape away plaque. Experiment to find your dog's favorite.

Why Do Puppies Chew?

Puppies chew because it teaches them life skills they need to learn. The chewing action also strengthens their muscles and helps them explore their world.

Chewing

Chewing is more than just a puppy habit. It is a necessary part of their physical and mental development. Chew toys are dragged around, fought over, and guarded with vocal warnings, all of which are life skills puppies need to learn. Their muscles are strengthened when engaging in these activities, too. Puppies also chew as a means of exploring their world. When they chew, they are developing their sense of taste to discern what is food and what isn't. They can't always rely on their eyes to tell the difference; some snakes can look much the same as electrical cords.

Puppies begin to lose their baby teeth around four months of

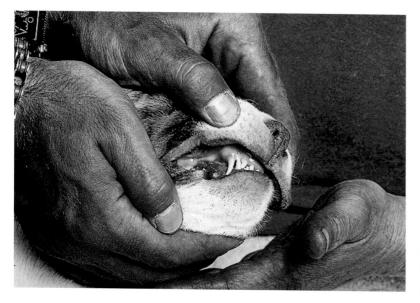

Examine your APBT's teeth regularly to promote good dental health.

age, and their adult teeth will replace them. As parents of human babies know, teething creates an urge to chew. For puppies, this is when their adult teeth are about to come in. The first replacement teeth are the front incisors, followed by the canine teeth (fangs). Sometimes the puppy tooth refuses to budge before the adult replacement erupts. This condition, called a *retained deciduous tooth*, can cause gum infections if debris and hair get trapped between the retained baby tooth and the adult tooth. Fortunately, the right kinds of chew toys can help prevent this.

How to Select the Best Chew Toys

There are so many chew toys available in stores; how do you know which ones are best for your APBT puppy? Puppies will chew on just about anything, but some toys are too easily torn apart and become choking hazards. Soft, rubbery squeaky toys are a prime example. Pups love the sound they make, but the soft material is easy to rend, and the squeaker mechanism can be swallowed. Beyond the choking hazard these toys present, swallowing them can cause injury as they make their way through the digestive system. The same goes for any kind of dog toy with buttons or other decorations. A puppy will pull them off with his mouth in the blink of an eye.

Hard, durable products are ideal chew toys for puppies.

Bad Breath Remedies

If your APBT's breath starts wilting dandelions, first see the vet to make sure that there is no underlying medical reason. If the cause is just plain old halitosis, you can try many ways to make him kissable again. Commercial canine breath fresheners come in just about every form, from hard chew treats to chlorophyll drops for his water bowl. If he has eaten something outside that is particularly nasty, offer him apple slices or fresh parsley. Both have odor-neutralizing qualities that eliminate bad breath.

These kinds of products massage gums and clean teeth, but they won't splinter or break or cause choking hazards. They come in bone shapes and other shapes, smooth or with a nubbly surface, flavored or unflavored. They are available in all sizes so that you can match the right size chew toy to your puppy's stage of growth.

Whatever chew toys you give your pup, check their condition periodically. Toys with sharp edges or rough spots from chewing can cut or chafe the inside of his mouth and should be replaced.

The Senior's Mouth

The act of chewing helps shed stubborn puppy teeth and massages the gums to promote the eruption of new teeth. Puppies with chew toys tend to be less destructive, develop more physically, and have less chance of retained deciduous teeth.

A lifetime of chewing with those strong jaws means that your APBT's teeth may need special care when he reaches his golden years. Check for tartar buildup on his teeth or sudden offensive breath. It may be time for a professional dental cleaning by the vet. This is performed under general anesthesia, enabling the vet to give a thorough cleaning. She will also look for any tooth or gum disease or chipped or cracked teeth that sometimes result from chewing hard bones or stones. Some dogs develop fibrous gum tumors that are harmless in themselves but can interfere with the dog's bite if allowed to proliferate. Bacteria can become lodged underneath the growths and cause infection. The vet will snip away these tumors while the dog is under general anesthesia. Bleeding and pain are minimal, and your APBT can resume eating the same day, sticking to soft foods for the next day or two.

Although there is some inherent risk with general anesthesia, the benefits of a professional dental cleaning far outweigh the minimal risk for a healthy dog. Unchecked oral problems can lead to infection, which if allowed to spread to internal organs, can cause serious illness or even death. A lifelong program of good dental hygiene will reduce the need for a professional cleaning and keep your APBT healthy and happy.

Good grooming is no substitute for poor physical fitness or ill health. If a dog is not well cared for, all the brushing in the world won't disguise it. Grooming is part of the responsibility a dog owner undertakes. APBT owners are luckier than most, though, because the APBT's low-maintenance coat enables his human to spend more time playing flyball and less time primping. And for you macho types who would rather not be caught hugging your APBT, don't worry. We'll just say you're checking for ticks.

Check your dog's chew toys periodically to make sure there are no sharp edges or rough spots.

TRAINING *and* BEHAVIOR

of Your American Pit Bull Terrier

I t has been said that living with an untrained dog is like owning a piano that you don't know how to play. It's nice to look at, but think of how much more rewarding it would be if you learned to make music with it. This is more than just a metaphor—it's a mandate. An untrained APBT is a potential menace who may live up to the breed's unsavory notoriety. A well-mannered APBT who is properly socialized and acknowledges his owner as leader of the pack, on the other hand, is an enjoyable, interesting dog to be with. The trained APBT is self-confident, the owner is proud, and both are devoted to each other.

THE IMPORTANCE OF TRAINING

Combine a strong, muscular dog with intelligence and curiosity and you get an APBT who needs training, even more so than other breeds. Without it, their brute strength and rough play could get them in all sorts of trouble. All dogs need training and socialization to help them learn about and cope with the world around them. This becomes even more important with a breed traditionally portrayed as vicious.

The APBT is in danger of becoming a disappearing breed, thanks to hostile media that continue to depict this wonderful dog as naturally aggressive and unpredictable. As long as "pit bulls" keep falling into the hands of people who encourage fighting and aggression, do not properly socialize or train, and indiscriminately breed their dogs, the APBT will continue to receive bad press. Thorough training is an APBT's best defense against such slander.

Responsible Dog Ownership

Responsible dog ownership includes keeping control of

your dog at all times. This is doubly true for APBT owners. Resolve to give your APBT puppy the best training available. If you adopt an older puppy or adult APBT, find out if he had received training while in his former home. If not, it may take a little more patience and persistence to unlearn bad habits, but it's imperative that the dog learn acceptable behavior. Owning an untrained APBT means, at best, owning a dog who will never reach his potential as a companion. At worst, it spells disaster. Imagine a powerful, uncontrollable dog in a social environment where he already has irrational fears about other dogs. The picture isn't pretty.

Finding a Reputable Trainer

The first order of business is to find a reputable trainer to work with you and your APBT. Yes, both of you. The training is as much for you as for your dog, because you will be practicing at home what you learn from the trainer. Look for one who suits your personality and philosophy.

Look for a trainer who suits your personality and training philosophy.

A good trainer will model her methods after the dog's first instructor—the mother dog. She taught her little APBTs many things while they were with her, and the instinctive tools she employed are useful patterns for you to follow. She was fair, consistent, immediate, and appropriate in her discipline. Above all, she always acted out of love. Even reprimands were carried out in a nurturing, loving context.

Enforcing Rules Consistently

Consistency is the key to successful dog training. The

rules you establish for your APBT should be respected and enforced by all the humans in the family, not just the one who takes him to obedience class. Get the kids involved; let them know they are an important part of the pet's adjustment to his new home. They need to understand not only the new pup's boundaries, but also their own as well.

To dispel the myths and reveal the true nature of these wonderful dogs, we have our work cut out for us. We need to show that APBTs make excellent family pets and that they can be trained well and developed into loyal, loving family protectors. We need to demonstrate that they can share their love as therapy dogs and successfully participate in dog sports. The breed's very survival may depend on how well we do this work.

Desire to Please

APBTs are so anxious to please that they are quite easily trained. The bond formed early between you and your APBT will go a long way in developing a relationship in which he knows what you expect of him and is happy to oblige.

BEFORE YOU TRAIN

A lot of pets go untrained because their owners equate obedience training with military boot camp, which is physically harsh and emotionally stressful. Training isn't about breaking your APBT's spirit; it's about helping him "be all that he can be."

Dogs are pack animals who find security in knowing their place in the pecking order. They also crave structure and enjoy having "work" to do, like weight pulling, agility competition, or just pleasing their owners by obeying simple commands. The best way to dispel the APBT's reputed viciousness is to show the world the smart, well-behaved, fun dog he really is.

Positive Training

Social animals like dogs and humans need discipline—and the education to learn to obey certain rules—to learn how to function successfully in the world. With dogs, especially APBTs, obedience is best achieved with the practice of positive reinforcement. You really do catch more flies with honey than with vinegar.

APBTs resent unfair, harsh behavior correction and will show it by refusing to move or even by fighting back. Obviously, you never want to antagonize an APBT to the point where he fights back. That's a poor training technique that puts you and others in danger.

APBTs are anxious-to-please dogs who will readily do your bidding if it culminates in praise, affection, or in the beginning, treats. Even when housetraining, praising him for going in the right place is much more effective than chastising him for going in the wrong place. APBTs are smart enough to quickly figure out what you want them to do.

Training Tools

Tools of the trade are important for any successful venture, and training your APBT is no different. You'll find that many dog training resources have many different recommendations on which tools are necessary, especially if selling a specific product is part of their advice. Unfortunately, much of the elaborate training paraphernalia is designed for restraint, correction, and punishment rather than for positive learning.

The tangible tools you need for successful training can be found in any store. We already have the most important tools within ourselves: love, patience, gentleness, and a good attitude. Add a willing APBT to the mix, and training will be a fun, fruitful experience.

Collar

Any kind of collar will feel strange to a puppy at first. He will paw and scratch at it, but before long he will get used to it. So many types are available; which do you buy?

For everyday use, an adjustable buckle collar is best. It should fit comfortably around the APBT's neck, not so loose that he can wriggle out of it, and not so tight that it constricts his throat. These flat nylon collars come in a wide variety of colors and styles, so you can go as fancy or as plain as you wish. For shows, try to match the color of the collar to the dog. Bright, contrasting colors distract the judge.

Opinions differ on which type of collar is best to start off your APBT's training, but the most popular choices seem to be the nylon show collar and the fine chain collar. (The chain collar can easily become caught on something and cause injury or even strangle the dog.) These should be used *only* for training sessions, and you should have a professional show you how to use them properly before choosing one over the other. Prong and pinch collars are not recommended, and in some areas, are not allowed.

Leash

It's important that you and your APBT feel comfortable with the leash, because he will need to be under your control at all times outside. A leather, nylon, or cotton-webbing training leash (also called a *lead*) that is about 6 feet (1.8 m) long is the most popular type for working with your APBT. Some leashes are made entirely of chain, but many dog handlers find them uncomfortable to work with. Retractable leashes are also a dubious choice for APBTs, whose great strength can snap the plastic mechanism if they take off after something.

A common mistake is to allow an APBT off-leash outdoors before you have established complete control. You may think

The leash is an essential training tool.

the APBT will obey your verbal command, but if he sees or smells a rabbit or other enticing creature, your training will fly out of his head. If you want to give your APBT some freedom but don't trust your verbal control, let him explore with the attached leash dragging behind. Stay close enough so that you can quickly pick it up and regain control if you have to.

Treats

Treats are a dog trainer's best friend. You can see in the show ring that even a well-trained dog often receives treats as rewards for a good performance. Trainers always have a stash of nutritious, easy-to-swallow treats on hand. Bits of hot dog, chunks of cheese, and pieces of cooked chicken all work best as training rewards.

Although treats are effective in

training, if you consistently reward good performance with them, your APBT may decide he won't perform without them. To avoid this problem, have him do certain commands twice before rewarding with a treat. Slowly increase the number of nonrewarded commands, and then vary them—two sits for a piece of cheese one day, four sits for a bite of hot dog the next day. Your APBT will realize that there is no set pattern to treat rewards and will probably do as you command the first time, hoping the reward will come sooner rather than later.

Treats can also be used to mark a certain behavior as soon as it happens. The APBT will soon learn to associate that behavior with a reward. He will repeat the behavior in the hope that you will dole out a delicious tidbit.

Some dog owners fear that treat rewards will encourage their APBT to beg at the table, but this is just not so. The only way to encourage a dog to beg at the table is to give him food from the table. Treat rewards should be given far away from the table. The dog will soon associate praise and tasty rewards with demonstrating behavior that pleases his owner.

Break Stick

APBT fanciers have no doubt heard the term *break stick* but may not have known what it is. Many think that every APBT owner should possess one. Read on and decide for yourself.

A break stick is about the size of a hammer handle and made of sturdy material like wood or fiberglass. One end is a handle and the other is flat and wedge-shaped. It is used to break the jaw hold of an APBT on another dog in the unfortunate event of a fight. The flat end is inserted into the corner of the APBT's mouth, then twisted to pry the jaws open and allow some leverage to pull him off the other dog, without injuring either dog.

Like the APBT breed itself, break sticks have a negative connotation because they are often associated with people who fight dogs. It also contributes to the myth that APBTs have locking jaws. But responsible APBT owners know that it can be a good tool to have on hand when the unexpected happens. A properly used break stick can separate two fighting dogs in a matter of seconds, greatly reducing likely injuries.

To break up a dog skirmish using a break stick, straddle the APBT from behind, clasping your knees around his waist. Use one hand to hold his head steady, either by the scruff of his neck or by his collar. With the other hand, insert the flat end of the break stick into the far corner of the dog's mouth, through the gap between the back of his jaw and his molars. Twist the stick and the dog's jaws will open their grip. As soon as you feel that you have leverage, pull the dogs apart.

Nothing is scarier than an accidental dog fight, and it helps to know what tools to use and how to safely break one up. Unfortunately, the break stick is too often considered part of dog-fighting paraphernalia. It can even be used as evidence against someone suspected of illegal activity, especially if more than one stick is found in the home. Too often, the real culprits are not discovered, and innocent, responsible APBT owners are challenged for having break sticks. For this reason, it's a good idea not to advertise the fact that you have a break stick. It doesn't add any cachet to owning an APBT and should be used for emergency purposes only, so there's no reason to brag about it.

Tips on Break Stick Usage

The following are some tips on how to use a break stick appropriately, without causing injury to yourself or your dog.

- Keep break sticks in a handy place that you can access quickly in the event of a fight, such as by the door to the back yard.
- Familiarize yourself with the stick and how to use it before you ever need to use it. A real dog fight is no time for on-the-job training.
- Realize that if the fight is between two APBTs, the break stick may not succeed in disengaging them. Have alternate methods available, such as a garden hose to douse them with water.
- Don't use a break stick on breeds other than the APBT. Their anatomy is different, and you might inadvertently injure the dog while trying to insert the stick.

SOCIALIZATION

The socialization your dog receives up to the age of three months will largely determine the impressions he develops about the outside world. A lack of socialization during puppyhood can manifest as a fearful or aggressive older dog. In addition, introducing a friendly, lovable APBT to the community goes a long way toward changing people's perception of the breed.

A puppy's socialization begins while he is still in his breeder's care, and it is up to you to continue this all-important process. It's one of the best things you will do for your APBT puppy, and it's fun for you, too.

Socializing your APBT while he is young will result in a well-behaved, well-adjusted adult.

How to Socialize

To socialize your dog, expose him to all kinds of people in all kinds of situations, as well as other animals. Allow him to interact with people of various races, ages, and genders, as well as people in wheelchairs, on crutches, and using walkers. Introduce him to other neighborhood pets, under your watchful eyes, of course.

Take your APBT out with you wherever possible to the park, to stores that welcome dogs, on a walk downtown—any safe place you normally visit during your everyday life. Keep in mind, though, that the world as a whole is still relatively new to this little guy. Although he should learn as much as he can about the world you both inhabit, very loud noises, large vehicles, and bright flashing lights can all be scary to him. Leave him in the security of his crate at home while you enjoy fireworks displays or demolition derbies. Even well-socialized adult dogs can become anxious in such environments.

Socializing your APBT puppy gives you a chance to show off your beautiful new family member, and your puppy gets to enjoy being an adorable little bundle that everyone will want to fuss over and find irresistible. Besides, after all the work involved in helping him adjust to his new home, you both deserve some fun social time.

CRATE TRAINING

Crate training involves acclimating your APBT to a safe place all his own where he can sleep, relax, and travel in security.

Unfortunately, the freedom fantasy has poisoned many people against the idea of crate training, and these people claim that such confinement is cruel and unnatural to social animals like dogs. Actually, their denning instinct facilitates crate training, and most dogs enjoy their crates, as long as they are a place of refuge, not of punishment. Make no mistake—leaving an unsupervised puppy unconfined puts his safety at great risk. Electric wires, poisonous houseplants, chemicals, and even furniture and staircases are all hazardous to an inquisitive little pup who regards everything as a chew toy. Crate training isn't cruel—it's the responsible thing to do.

Benefits of Crate Training

When a puppy is about 5 weeks old, he will start toddling away from his mother and littermates to relieve himself. The instinct not to soil his living area will be useful in the housetraining of your puppy. With the help of a crate, the process will be that much easier.

By taking advantage of his instinct not to soil his canine condo, your new puppy will learn more quickly where you want him to relieve himself. But at the tender age of ten weeks—when most puppies leave their litters for new homes—his developing bladder and bowel control will not allow him to go more than an hour or so without relieving himself. It is up to you to make sure he isn't left inside his crate too long.

Socializing Your APBT

The importance of socialization cannot be overemphasized, but it must be done early to be effective. Once your APBT puppy has had all his shots, here are some ideas for socializing him:

- Visit the kennel where he was born.
- Take him out in public to meet people of all genders, ages, and ethnicities.
- Allow children of different age groups to play with him, under careful adult supervision.
- Take him to parks and shops that welcome dogs.
- Introduce him to people who use canes, walkers, and wheelchairs.
- Expose him to bicycle and motorcycle riders, inline skaters and skateboarders, or even people riding horses.
- Familiarize him with his environment. In a rural setting, introduce him to farm animals. In a city, acquaint him with elevator rides and walking in crowds amid traffic noise.
- Take him to any competitive events in which you might later participate.

There will be times you are unable to supervise your puppy, even while at home. At these times, the crate will prevent him from soiling all over the house. It will also keep him out of mischief; you want him to be safe from potential hazards while you are unable to watch him.

Crate Location

The location of the crate goes a long way toward a decent night's sleep for both you and your puppy. Try placing it in your bedroom near the bed. Having you nearby will give the puppy a sense of security and reduce his crying. If you hear him whining or scratching at the crate door in the middle of the night, he most likely needs to go to the bathroom. Taking him outside at these times will speed up the housetraining process and bring you closer to that night of undisturbed sleep. Praise him when he does his business, and then put him back into the crate.

During the day, when your puppy looks tired, put him in the crate for a nap with the door shut. This will help him learn that the crate is the place to sleep.

Crate Size

Most dogs enjoy their crates, as long as they are a place of refuge, not of punishment.

Size does matter, for two reasons. Although he will eventually grow into a large dog, and you will need a size-appropriate crate, you don't want to start off with a large one while your APBT is still very young. If the crate is too large, your puppy will quickly discover that he can eliminate at one end of the crate and still have quite a bit of unsoiled bedding space. It is better to start with a smaller crate and upsize as he grows. A good rule of thumb when crate shopping is that it should be large enough for the dog to stand up and turn around in comfortably. If you must start with a larger size crate, partition off half of it to reduce the available space.

How to Crate Train

It may take a little while for your puppy to recognize the crate as his own special refuge. This is why it is a good idea to introduce the crate to him before you actually need to confine him in it.

Prepare the crate by lining the bottom with thick layers of newspaper to act as a cushion and absorb accidents. Prop open the crate door and toss a treat inside, saying, "Crate" or "Bed" as you do this. Allow him to go inside for the treat, sniff around a bit, and exit the crate when he is ready. Leave the door open to allow him to come and go as often as he wishes.

Dog crates are made of either plastic or wire and serve as a bed, travel cage, dining room, and safe place your pup can call his own.

When he seems comfortable with it, serve his next meal inside the crate. Keep the door open when he eats, and then progress to closing the door once he has gone inside to eat. When he is finished, let him out of the crate and immediately take him outside to relieve himself. Soon he will learn that the crate isn't a prison but a cozy nook where good things are to be had.

The hard part comes at bedtime. Your new APBT will no doubt cry the first night or two that he goes to bed alone in his crate. This is normal. After all, until now, he has spent his sleeping hours surrounded by the comfort of his littermates. Resist the temptation to let him out of the crate when he cries. Say, "Quiet!" in a firm voice or simply close the door to the room and leave. If you give in to his crying and let him out, he will learn that tantrums yield positive results. You want him to learn that he may come out of the crate only when he is quiet and you are ready.

HOUSETRAINING

Teaching your APBT where it is appropriate to relieve himself begins as soon as you bring him home. Don't expect too much from him, though, because his bladder and bowels are still immature. Puppies also mature at varying rates, meaning that some require more time than others to learn. So be patient!

How to Housetrain

Preparation for housetraining begins by bringing home in a sealable plastic bag some urine-soaked litter from your dog's living area at the breeder. Scatter the used litter around the outdoor site where your pup will relieve himself at home. The

scent will identify the site to him as the proper place to go.

Upon arriving home with your new pup, go immediately to the outdoor elimination site. Put him down where you've spread the litter, and wait patiently until he urinates and/or defecates. (This may take some time.) Lavish praise on him when he does. Convince him that he has just performed the greatest feat ever, and you couldn't be more pleased.

As you and your APBT settle into your life together, keep an eye out for telltale signals that he needs to go. If he walks around sniffing the floor, he is searching for the scent that tells him he's found the right place to eliminate. Take him outside right away and praise him when he goes. Always take him outside after eating, drinking, or sleeping, cheering him on when he relieves himself in the correct spot.

Accidents

It's a fact of life: Accidents will happen. When it does, never punish your APBT by striking him or rubbing his nose in his mistake. This only conveys to him that you are displeased because he eliminated, not because he did so in the wrong place. He will learn to distrust you, something you don't want to foster.

If you catch the puppy in the act of soiling inside the house, take him immediately outside to finish the job. He may need a few extra minutes, as the interruption can be distracting. When he is finished, give lots of praise to show your approval of *this* elimination site.

If you discover an accident after the fact, it's too late for damage control. If you chastise the puppy now, he won't understand why. Clean up the mess right away with a product made especially to neutralize the scents in urine and feces, and resolve to keep a sharper eye on the puppy.

Ordinary home cleaning products will kill germs, but they do nothing to eliminate the scent that identifies the area as an acceptable place to go. If you have carpet and aren't sure where accidents have happened, invest in a black light from a pet supply store. In a completely dark room, the black light will reflect even old urine stains and show you just where the accidents took place.

Remember, if your puppy has an accident in the house, it's

not his fault but yours. Somewhere along the line, you slipped up on supervision. Don't scold him; just clean up the mess and move on. It may take his bladder a month or two before he can "hold it" very long, but he will understand quickly where you want him to go. With patience and consistency, your APBT puppy can be housetrained in short order.

LEASH TRAINING

Leash training is one of the first things you both should learn, especially if you plan to participate with your APBT in conformation shows. A good time to begin is when your puppy has enough stamina for short walks, at around the age of seven weeks. By that age, his attention span will have also increased to the point where he will benefit from mental stimulation, and leash training is just the ticket.

To teach your APBT how to walk nicely on a lead, you must first teach the puppy to follow you off-lead. Start walking him in a calm, enclosed area, allowing him to explore. While he's happily sniffing around, show him a treat and call him to come close to you. Praise him when he does, and reward him with the treat. Encourage him to follow you as you walk for a few minutes, and then release him to explore some more on his own. The goal here is to acquaint him with walking by your side off-lead so that the transition to walking on-lead will be easy.

After he has gotten the hang of following you off-lead, it's time to move to walking on-lead. Begin in an area the puppy has come to know well, like your own yard. The familiar smells will help him stay focused on the training session. New scents are just too tempting for a puppy to resist! Attach the lead to his collar and begin walking. Call him to you, enticing him with a treat, and he should follow you the same way he did off-lead.

An alternate method is to attach the lead to the pup's collar, and then back away from him with a treat in your hand. Stoop down and offer him the treat as you tell him to come. This sends a dual message—that coming to his owner when called *and* following her will reap tasty rewards.

BASIC OBEDIENCE TRAINING

Ideally, obedience training begins before you even bring your new puppy home. Because you have made a conscious decision

Paper Training

Some people prefer to start housetraining their APBT with paper training. This makes sense for city or apartment dwellers who don't have ready access to an outside elimination spot. It's best, however, to skip the paper training when possible and go directly into outdoor potty training, because the intermediate step of paper training can be confusing to the dog. (He might have trouble understanding that he's supposed to potty outside after mastering paper training.)

Lavish praise on your APBT puppy when he eliminates in the correct place.

to add an APBT to your family, it's a given that you have read up on the breed and talked to professionals about the specific needs of an APBT. Basic obedience is more than important for this breed—it is crucial. And the crucial time to learn basic obedience is during the first few weeks at home, so you need to be prepared.

Use Positive Reinforcement

It is worth repeating that positive reinforcement for desired behavior, not punishment for mistakes, is the key to successful training. Punishment is not only confusing and ineffective, but it is unfair. Why punish the dog for doing something wrong before he even learns what is right?

Keep Training Sessions Short

Puppies have limited attention spans, so keep the early training sessions short, about ten minutes or so. Put him through several separate sessions throughout the day; repetition is crucial. Older dogs may remember an action after only a couple of demonstrations, but puppies don't have long memories. As he grows, and you move on to more advanced training, the lessons can be longer.

Form Goals

Before you embark on a training program, think about what

your goals are for your APBT. Do you want a well-mannered, calm homebody? Do you want him to be well behaved beyond immediate family and home turf? Do you aspire to dog sports and competitions? Once you have a clear idea of where you and your dog are headed, you can find a training program to help you achieve those goals.

Teach the Basic Five

The first commands your APBT will master are *sit, stay, heel, come,* and *down.* Because your priority is total control of your APBT at all times, these commands work well to that end. And of course, a well-mannered dog is always preferable to an undisciplined, hyperactive pet.

In addition to making your APBT a more delightful dog to be around, obeying the basic five commands could well save his life someday. An APBT dashing through an open door after a

Begin teaching your dog to walk on a leash in an area he knows well, like your yard.

squirrel won't care that he's in the path of an oncoming car. Your command to stay or to come may be the only thing that saves him from being hit. Or suppose your leashed APBT meets up with an unleashed dog, and bad vibes begin to build. If an argument seems to be a distinct possibility, you won't necessarily have the physical strength to pull your dog away, leash or no leash. An APBT trained to ignore signs of aggression from other dogs will not engage in an argument, saving the dogs from injury and you from legal woes.

Sit

The simple *sit* is invariably the first

Most dogs learn to sit very quickly.

command a dog will learn. It is a good place to start, because the puppy already knows how to do it. The trick is to get him to do it when *you* want him to do it. No matter how slowly he might pick up on other commands, if you end each training session with a nicely executed *sit*, followed by a reward, you'll keep his confidence up and keep obedience training a happy experience.

In preparation for a training session, put on your APBT's training collar and leash. Hold the leash in your left hand and a food treat in your right. Hold your hand with the treat by your dog's nose, and allow him to lick the treat but not take it. You're just showing him the incentive at this point. Next, slowly raise your food hand from in front of his nose upward to over his head. He will automatically assume a *sit* position as his eyes and head raise to follow the treat. Give the verbal command, "Sit!" at precisely the same moment that his head goes up and his rear goes down. Give him the treat and lavish praise on him.

APBTs love nothing better than making their humans happy, so your dog will quickly get the hang of this command. Once he does, wean him away from food treats when he sits on command, but keep up the hearty praise. There will come a time in his life when you do not have treats with you, but you need your dog to obey.

Stay

The *stay* is arguably the most crucial command of the basic five commands. Don't skimp on teaching this one; the *stay* could keep your dog out of a serious altercation and could even save his life. The challenge is teaching this command to a puppy who wants to stay by your side every minute. During leash training, you have also taught him to follow you. How do you now tell him that he must be at some distance from you and remain there?

Begin with the leashed puppy in a *sit* next to your left leg. Have a treat in your right hand, and place that hand at your APBT's nose. Tell him, "Stay," making a "stop" gesture with the open right palm in front of his face. Step forward with your right foot and stand directly in front of the dog. Let him lick the treat in your hand, and keep his head facing upward to maintain the *sit* position. Count to five, and then turn back around to stand next to your dog again, with him on your left. As soon as you are back in your original position, give him the treat and lots of praise. He stayed, even if it was for only five seconds.

However, if the dog steps out of his *sit* position when you move away, as he probably will, stop him and start the lesson over by putting him back in a *sit* position. He may not get this one right away, because it combines the use of verbal and hand signals, but try not to get frustrated. Keep the practice sessions short, and always end with a *sit*, praise, and a treat.

As your APBT becomes adept at the *stay* command, you can gradually increase the time you ask him to hold the position. Keep in mind, though, that if he is not holding the *stay* and is moving too much, you might be asking him to hold it for too long. If this is the case, go back to the beginning and reteach the basic *stay*.

Heel

Heeling occurs when a dog walks beside his human without pulling. Because of the APBT's natural strength, heel is an important command to learn. You want to be walking the dog instead of the dog walking you. It may take some time for him to understand fully that you will not proceed unless he is calmly heeling.

Pre-heeling training begins right away, when the young puppy learns to follow his master while walking off-leash. When he is ready to progress to on-leash walking, you are ready to begin teaching the *heel*.

To teach *heel*, first put your pup in the *sit* position, next to your left foot. With the leash in your left hand, step off with your left foot. As you make the first step, say, "Heel." If he does not step forward as you do, get him moving by slapping the coils of extra leash against your leg as you keep walking. Walk together about three steps, stop, and then tell him to sit. Praise him verbally, holding your position as he holds his. After a moment, say, "Heel" again, and take three more steps. Stop again and have your dog sit.

As long as he stays by your left leg while walking, praise him. If he stops or veers away, stop walking and start the lesson over. Your immediate goal is to have him walk calmly beside you for three steps without him pulling on the leash. When he has mastered heeling for three steps, advance to five. Keep increasing the number of steps you take with him heeling until he understands that leash walking means heeling. Sometimes a particularly stubborn dog will continue pulling on his leash. If your APBT is one of them, stand still and do not move until he stops pulling and resumes the proper *heeling* position. Eventually, he will get the message.

What Is Heeling?

Heeling occurs when a dog walks beside his human without pulling.

Keep the lessons short, and let your APBT know that the lesson is finished by praising and petting him. It should only take a few days before he is heeling like a pro.

Down

This command requires the puppy to lie down on his belly and stay there. Initially, he may feel vulnerable in this position, so you must take care to use the proper method of teaching him *down*.

With training collar and lead attached, put the dog in a *sit* position. Hold the leash in your left hand and a treat in your right. Rest one hand lightly on top of his shoulders. Do not push down on his back; just let your hand rest there to guide him close to your side when he lies down. Move your right hand in front of his nose and say, "Down" very quietly, slowly lowering the treat to his front feet. When your hand reaches the floor, keep it moving forward along the floor in front of the dog. He will try to follow the food hand by lowering himself to the floor. Talk softly to him all the while, because your reassuring voice will calm him.

When the dog's elbows reach the floor, give him the treat and soft praise. Try to keep him in the *down* position for a few seconds. Everything should be done in a soothing, easy way to reassure the dog. If you pull the treat away too far and too fast, he will stand up instead of lie down. If you push your hand down on his body and speak harshly, he will feel threatened and unwilling to obey. Be patient until he does what you want. When he is comfortable with the command, take the treat out of the scenario but continue using your right hand for a signal. Eventually, he will know that the downward hand movement, coupled with the verbal command, means "hit the deck."

Teaching the dog to obey the *down* command from a standing position is not very different from the *sit* position. Say, "Down," and lower the hand with the treat to the floor. He will lower his forelegs into a play bow, at which point you can slowly move the treat on the floor toward his legs. As soon as the rear end is down, give the treat and lots of praise.

Come

Surprisingly, the *come* command is more involved than you might guess. True, it takes little time to get your APBT to come to you when called, because most puppies gladly approach everyone, whether summoned or not. When they hit doggy adolescence, though, distractions such as tantalizing odors on the grass take precedence over coming when their humans call. Fortunately, *come* is easily taught, but it can be just as easily untaught if misapplied.

You can teach your puppy to come in two simple ways. The first involves putting the puppy on a long lead while you stand at the far end of it. Gradually gather the leash in your hands to bring him toward you, while calling, "Come!" He will no doubt trot happily toward you, so start praising him as soon as he starts to move. Even if he gets distracted before he reaches you and veers off toward something else, praise the steps he did take as you gave the command to come. Most of the time he will successfully reach you, and literally every step in the right direction deserves praise. Always reinforce positive actions, however brief they are.

Another method of teaching *come* is to kneel down, hold your arms wide open, and enthusiastically call, "Come!" Praise your puppy to the skies when he does. You won't need to use a treat to lure him, but you can use one to teach him that *come* doesn't mean *come knock me over*. When a rapidly approaching puppy is about three lengths away from mowing you down, give the *sit*

The down *command asks your dog to lie down on his belly and stay there.*

command with the treat in an outstretched hand. When your dog stops to check out the treat, move your food hand upward over his muzzle to put him in a *sit*. (If he jumps up for the treat, you're holding your hand too high.) Put him back in a *sit* before repeating the *come* exercise.

There are a few important points to remember about this command:

- *Never* call your APBT to you and then punish him. Association of the command with anything negative unravels all training progress in one fell swoop.
- Don't overwork the command by calling him to yourself too frequently.
- Spring an unexpected *come* on him when he is distracted by another activity, such as playing. You want him to learn to heed your call no matter what else he might be doing.
- Remember to always reward him for coming to you, whether it is with a treat or very enthusiastic praise.

Clicker Training

Voice commands have long been the most common training tool, but they are by no means the only one. Many dog enthusiasts favor clicker training, a method of positive reinforcement first used by dolphin trainers. Clicker training focuses on fostering a certain behavior, not stopping it. The clicker makes an identifiable sound that is used as a signal to mark a desired behavior as soon as it occurs, followed right away by a treat. Very soon, the dog learns that the clicker sound means that a reward is in his immediate future, and that he can get you to make the clicking sound by repeating the marked behavior. The advantage here is that the clicker pinpoints exactly what behavior results in the reward and provides the dog with consistent, unemotional information. In addition, because the clicking noise is different from other environmental signals, it encourages him to focus.

Special-needs dogs can benefit from clicker training, too. Substitute the clicker with a light flash to train a deaf dog. A fearful dog can gain confidence from clicker training, and it is highly effective in calming the aggressive dog. Clicker training involves little human–dog contact, so a shy APBT won't feel threatened during the positive-response clicker method. Soft voices and light touches are employed to soothe the dog and build trust. No negative action is taken by the trainer to trigger the dog's fear response. The clicker method also works well with aggressive dogs, because it is used to sidestep any aggressive reaction. The dog is trained to calm down when he hears the click and gets a treat. Eventually, he will know when a command requires him to calm down, and he won't even need the clicker. This doesn't happen overnight, but clicker training can create a positive emotional state and turn a once-aggressive dog into a great family pet.

Many shelter-adopted or rescued APBTs were given up because of problem behaviors. Clicker training is a great way to integrate such a dog into a new home and address any behavioral issues.

Did You Know?

The clicker marks a desired behavior as soon as it occurs, which is followed immediately by a treat.

FORMAL TRAINING CLASSES

The APBT's high intelligence level and desire to please make him a very trainable dog, but in inexperienced hands, he may not get the training he needs to function in a society that looks askance at the breed. Sure, you could teach your APBT how to sit and heel, but will you be confident that he will stay when commanded or calm down in the face of potential dog aggression? Unless you are an experienced dog trainer who has worked with APBTs before, you are better off enrolling in a

The Five Basics

Whichever training method you decide to use, be aware of the five basics you need to master in order to set up your APBT for success:

1. Make corrections immediately.
2. Be consistent.
3. Be patient.
4. Reward and praise with enthusiasm.
5. Don't lose your temper.

APBTs live to please you. They will become enthusiastic partners in their own obedience training, making it fun for both of you.

formal training program, whether for private instruction or group classes.

No matter which training environment you choose, be sure there's a good fit between you, your dog, and the instructor. Observe different classes to see if you and your APBT will be comfortable with that instructor's methods.

- Are the dogs in the class enjoying themselves?
- Does the instructor handle the dogs in a way you would want your APBT handled?
- Are the dogs and humans paying attention to the instructor?

Group Classes

Consider the pros and cons of group classes versus private obedience instruction. In a group, the dog must learn how to behave around distractions, namely the other dogs and people in the class. Considering that you want your APBT to remain in your control at all times, no matter what distractions occur, this might be a good choice for you. Your dog may even find some future playmates among his classmates. The downside of group classes is that the distractions sometimes prove too much for certain dogs.

Private Lessons

For dogs who have trouble concentrating, individual lessons might be in order. Sometimes, a few private lessons are all that the dog needs to join a group class later. For obvious reasons, one-on-one lessons are better for dogs with aggression or other behavioral problems. Private lessons may also be the only type of training busy dog owners can fit into their schedules.

Puppy Classes

Puppy or "kindergarten" classes for puppies between 10 and 16 weeks of age are part obedience training, part socialization. Owners also learn how to prevent problem behaviors and how to establish boundaries. APBT puppies benefit greatly from kindergarten classes.

PROBLEM BEHAVIORS

The intelligence, tenacity, and resourcefulness that make the APBT such an enjoyable breed are the same qualities that can cause problems if you aren't prepared for them. Many of the behaviors we consider troublesome—barking, digging, chewing, and jumping up on people—aren't problems to your APBT. On the contrary—they come very naturally. Fortunately, though, problem behaviors can be addressed and controlled once the underlying causes are identified.

Common Problem Behaviors

- aggression
- barking
- begging
- coprophagia
- digging
- food stealing
- jumping up
- mounting
- separation anxiety

Aggression

APBTs are not usually aggressive toward humans, but they can display a natural aggression toward other dogs. From the age of nine months, the APBT could develop a desire to test his strength against others. Thus, from puppyhood on, socialization with other dogs is crucial to reduce the impulse to challenge others. APBTs can and should be trained to ignore other dogs, even when challenged. Done early and properly, this training will help the APBT realize that other dogs pose no threat.

Aggression is more than just ill-mannered behavior; it can be downright dangerous, especially with a powerful, determined APBT. The saddest situation is one in which an APBT family becomes afraid of their dog's unpredictable temperament. While all aggression doesn't necessarily result in injury, it must be dealt with immediately.

Solution

To effectively deal with aggression, you must first get to the root of the behavior and find out why your APBT thinks he should be leader of the pack. How can you tell if your APBT thinks he is in charge? Observe his body language. Telltale signals let you know when a dog is about to challenge. Does he make direct eye contact and stare? Does he try to make himself appear as large as possible: tail held high, chest out, ears up and out? These signs indicate that the dog thinks he is literally above the rest, and top-dog mentality can lead to unpredictable behavior.

Sometimes aggression originates in fear. The "fight or flight" instinct kicks in, and the brave APBT stands up to whatever is scaring him. Fear in a grown dog often results from poor socialization during puppyhood or is the result of a traumatic experience. If you can isolate the cause of your dog's fear, you can recondition his reaction to it. Pay close attention to all his interactions with people and other dogs, and praise him when everything goes well. At the first sign of rising aggression, correct him verbally and take him away from the situation.

Do not allow anyone to approach and pet your APBT without your permission. This will allow you to put your dog in a *sit*, ready to accept the attention. Praise him when he behaves appropriately. Positive reinforcement and gentle supervision put

The APBT's high intelligence level and desire to please make him a very trainable dog.

you on the path to modifying aggressive behavior. The dog will soon see he has nothing to be afraid of, so there is no need to be defensive.

Dogs who are in pain or who are injured often bite out of fear, which is understandable. You will most likely know if your dog is hurting—if he is limping, licking a wound, or bleeding—but sometimes injuries are not readily visible. A complete veterinary examination will reveal or rule out any physical causes of uncharacteristic aggression.

If your APBT continues to behave aggressively, and your veterinarian has ruled out any physical cause, don't despair. Severe or chronic aggression is not always a death sentence. Professionals are available to help you;

start networking in your community to find them. The best consultant is a veterinarian who specializes in dog behavior or a trainer experienced with problem dogs. If you can find someone experienced in APBT behavior, so much the better. Ask for referrals from professional organizations like the American Animal Hospital Association (AAHA) or the Endangered Breed Association (EBA).

Barking

Barking is the only way dogs have of talking. It is not always easy to tell what they are trying to say with their barks, which can be frustrating. Is your dog happy, scared, angry? It takes time to become familiar with the different qualities of your dog's bark in different situations.

Whatever the message is, your APBT should never be punished for barking. Sometimes, you definitely want him to vocalize, such as if an intruder is in your home. The problem is that a dog cannot differentiate when it is appropriate to bark from when it is inappropriate. He won't understand why he's a good dog for barking at a possible intruder but a bad dog for barking when the mailman comes to the door. All he knows is that someone is approaching his turf and you should know about it, be it friend or foe. Only when barking becomes excessive and habitual is behavior modification in order—and the earlier the better.

Solution

APBTs are not typically problem barkers, but a dog who is left alone every day for long stretches of time may discover that barking brings attention, even if it is a neighbor yelling at him to stop. (Dogs do not distinguish between positive and negative attention.)

To help curb excessive barking, encourage your APBT to be quiet at home with you. If he begins barking for no good reason, tell him, "Quiet!" and reward him when he stops.

When your APBT has learned this command, it is time to take the next step. Go outside for a solitary walk around the block, and listen for any barking when you leave and return. Make your exits and entrances unemotional so that your dog does not bark out of excitement. If you do hear him barking in

Although APBTs are not usually aggressive toward humans, they can display a natural aggression toward other dogs.

protest of your departure, come back and correct him with another "Quiet!" and a treat for calming down. Take the training further still by asking a neighbor to come talk to you outside. If the dog barks because he feels left out, correct him. Repeat these steps as often as necessary until he learns not to bark.

Begging

What dog wouldn't want a bite of our dinner, with all the delicious smells wafting by his nose? And we might be inclined to indulge our dogs if begging didn't quickly develop into an annoying habit.

Begging is a conditioned response to a certain stimulus, time, or place. The sounds of food preparation in the kitchen, cans being opened, sizzling meat, the clink of silverware, or even the approach of the dinner hour can start making your dog's mouth water. Give in just one time to his request for a handout, and he'll be back for more. If he doesn't get it, he may start whining, drooling, pawing at you, and even plaintively resting his chin on your lap.

Solution

APBTs know exactly who the softies are, so resolve as a family not to give in to begging. It may get worse before it gets better, but eventually it will stop.

Dogs don't become beggars; people create them. They are also responding to a survival instinct that tells them to grab whatever food they can, whenever they can. In a breed like the APBT, food gulping in a situation like this could even bring about gastric torsion (bloat), a fatal condition unless treated immediately. The bottom line is that you shouldn't feel bad when you deny the begging dog; you are doing him a favor by breaking a bad habit.

Coprophagia

Coprophagia, or the eating of feces, is a good candidate for the title of "Most Disgusting Dog Behavior"—disgusting to humans, that is. To a dog, this behavior is perfectly acceptable.

Coprophagia usually refers to the dog eating his own feces, but it also refers to the consumption of another animal's feces. Oddly enough, coprophagic dogs often prefer cat or horse stool over the feces of another dog. Deer droppings are a real delicacy to some dogs. The consistency of the stool and the presence of undigested nutrients make a difference; dogs seem to prefer eating harder stools.

Why would a dog eat feces? He may be seeking certain nutrients that are missing in his diet, he could simply be hungry, or he might be drawn to the pleasing scent. Instinct may also tell him to get rid of the evidence so as not to attract predators.

Coprophagia usually results in diarrhea, which would likely make your dog kick the habit of eating his own feces. But you can take active steps to eliminate the behavior.

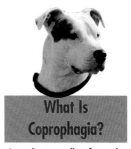

What Is Coprophagia?

Coprophagia usually refers to the dog eating his own feces, although it also refers to the consumption of another animal's feces.

Solution

The first thing the coprophagic dog owner should do is make sure her dog's diet is nutritionally complete. Veterinarians have found that diets that are low in fiber and high in starch may increase coprophagia, so adding fiber is worth a try. Consult with your vet to make sure that no other medical reason is behind the behavior.

If your dog is physically fine but continues to eat feces, behavior modification through environmental control is the next step. Commercial products are available that you can feed your dog or sprinkle on his food that render the feces unpalatable without changing the taste of the food. The best solution, though, is to make animal feces unavailable. Clean up waste from your fenced-in yard. If you catch your dog in the act, distract him rather than reprimand him, because a rebuke rarely works.

Fortunately, coprophagia is most often seen in puppies six

months to a year old, and it usually resolves itself around the dog's first birthday.

Digging

Digging is viewed by humans as a destructive behavior, but it really is a natural one. Dogs love to dig, especially terriers, whose job historically has been to ferret out vermin. We often forget that, in domesticating dogs, we have taken away from them the burden of finding food and making shelter. In the wild, these pursuits would constructively occupy the dogs' time, energy, and paws. Because we provide food and comfort for them, this unchanneled energy may be manifested in holes all over the yard and flower beds.

It is not just instinct at work here. Dirt and soil are unending sources of tempting smells that make digging great fun. Your APBT may also dig out of boredom.

Solution

Digging is a tough behavior to correct because it is difficult to catch a dog in the act. Dog owners are usually away from home or busy inside the house when their dogs are digging. By the time they notice the holes, it is too late to chastise the dog, because the

To prevent your APBT from digging, make sure that he gets plenty of exercise and playtime to keep him from becoming bored.

dog will not connect your reprimand with something he did ten hours earlier. You are left with a twofold problem: a torn-up yard and figuring out a way to contain your dog.

A determined APBT can dig under a fence to escape, and a free-ranging APBT is much worse than landscaping woes. Thus, the first thing you should do is to reinforce your fence with barriers below the ground that will prevent him from escaping.

Also, be sure your APBT gets plenty of exercise and playtime to stave off boredom. A contented, tired dog won't dig just because there is nothing better to do.

Another solution is to create a digging space for him that is his alone. If your APBT is a compulsive digger, it may be easier to work with the problem than it is to fight it. Fence off a section of your yard alongside your house, maybe 6 feet (1.8 m) by 20 feet (6.1 m). When you can't closely supervise him, let him dig there to his heart's content. When you *are* closely supervising, he can have free rein in the rest of your yard. If he starts to dig in the wrong place, use your voice to interrupt him. Just don't let him watch you gardening!

Food Stealing

It doesn't take dogs long to figure out that their owners keep the really good stuff for themselves. Just when you think you have positioned that steak far enough back on the kitchen countertop, your APBT once again proves that you underestimated him. APBTs are clever, tenacious food thieves who gleefully rise to the challenge. If you are losing too many packages of hot dogs to him, you need to address the issue.

Solution

To discourage food stealing, you must take the fun out of the behavior by making his reward less rewarding. Plant a shaker can (an empty soda can with coins or pebbles inside) on the counter with the food temptation. Place it so that it falls when he pulls down the food. Your dog will associate the startling noise with the item that he is stealing and look for his thrills elsewhere.

You can also buy inexpensive training tools that are really

Body Language and Communication

You can tell a lot from a dog's body language, and when dealing with a strong APBT, it's especially important that nothing gets lost in translation.

Body Language	What It Means
Dog looks at you sideways with a lowered head.	"I'm worried and unsure of your next move."
Dog stares at you with an elevated head, standing on tiptoes.	"I'm equal to the challenge and ready to pounce."
Front half of dog's torso is lowered in a bow.	"Let's play!"
Dog's entire body crouched, with tail hanging down and ears folding back.	"I submit to you."
Dog's lips curled back and fangs exposed.	"Watch out!"
Fur down the center of dog's back standing on end.	"I'm afraid but ready to defend myself."

Dogs also use vocalization to communicate. Barking at a higher-than-normal pitch means "I'm frustrated" or "I see something unfamiliar and I'm excited" or "Hurry up and come play!" Growling can be aggressive or playful, and it isn't hard to tell the difference. The dog's mood will be obvious. "Play growls" are usually low-pitched and rolling. Aggressive growling sounds similar but is accompanied by bared teeth and a menacing stance.

nothing more than motion-sensor devices. Place the monitor on the counter or table where the food is. It will emit a loud, startling noise when your dog gets too close or touches the device. This is also helpful for the sneaky APBT who likes to snooze on the forbidden couch when his humans are out.

Jumping Up

APBTs are people puppies. Visitors to your home will never have to wonder where they stand when meeting your dog. Like a child who is so excited he can't sit still, an APBT's enthusiasm often manifests in jumping on people. Very few people mind an adorable puppy jumping up in friendly greeting, but puppies grow up fast, and even die-hard dog lovers won't relish a 70-pound (31.8 kg) APBT bowling them over when they walk through the door, not to mention the havoc paws and claws can wreak on clothing.

Solution

Jumping up can be controlled by implementing the *sit* command. When you come home from work or another absence, don't greet your APBT pup until you have a leash and collar in your hand. It will be hard to ignore this wriggling bundle who is so happy to see you, but resist the impulse to scoop him up and let him slather your face with kisses. As he greets you, slip on the collar and tell him to sit. If he jumps up, tell him firmly, "No!" and give the *sit* command again. (Avoid saying, "Down!" as a correction for jumping, because you are already using that word to teach him to lie down.) Praise him when he obeys. He will learn that anything enjoyable happens only after he assumes the *sit* position.

Get in the habit of requiring your dog to sit before you serve his meals, before you pet him, before you attach his leash for a walk, or before anything he finds pleasurable. You are essentially teaching him the canine equivalent of saying "please" before indulging. If he sits for an approaching visitor, he knows that praise and attention will follow. Enlist the help of your guests by asking them not to pet the dog until he sits, so that he isn't inadvertently "rewarded" for incorrect behavior.

When out in public, your APBT is sure to attract attention, and many people will want to interact with him. Make him sit

If your APBT jumps up, use the sit *command to control the behavior.*

before allowing anyone to pet him. You may need to explain to people that you are trying to teach him good manners and that he must sit before getting any attention from people. Setbacks can occur if he jumps on someone and is then petted even once. The dog may decide the possibility of receiving attention is worth the risk of behaving incorrectly.

Mounting

Mounting here refers to the behavior, not the sexual act. Males and females alike are known to mount, and neutering does not necessarily eliminate this behavior. It is most often directed toward humans and other dogs but is also known to involve objects like pillows or stuffed animal toys.

People typically attribute mounting to sexual arousal or an attempt to establish or reinforce dominance, but that is usually not the reason. Dogs are hyperactive creatures, so mounting often occurs in situations in which the dog is (nonsexually) stimulated or excited. This is called *social overture during play*. It happens more with adolescent, small dogs (ahem, terriers!) and often stops on its own after the dog has matured.

Mounting can also be a sign of a dog's insecurity of his own position within the pack—you, your family, or other dogs in the home. He may be unsure where he stands in the pecking order and is attempting to reinforce it by mounting. If the dog being mounted submits to it, he's saying he knows who's boss. A growling, negative reaction means "back off; you're not my superior." A confident dog may just ignore the mounting, which means "I'm not impressed." Fortunately, you can avoid dominance insecurity with solid leadership from the time your dog is young.

Solution

If mounting behavior becomes a problem, try using the age-old tactic that mothers of crying toddlers have relied on since time immemorial: distraction. First, gently remove the dog from the mounting posture and say, "No!" sharply. If he tries to get right back in the saddle, give him something else to do that will calm him down without rewarding the mounting behavior. For example, practice a few obedience skills like *sit* and *down*. Alternatively, give him a time-out—take him aside and calm him down by talking soothingly. If all else fails, send the mounting dog to his crate. Let him know that this is not a punishment by putting a treat or a toy inside. If the behavior continues well into the dog's adulthood, seek advice from your veterinarian. It is possible that a hormonal issue needs to be addressed.

Mounting is sometimes nothing more than a style of play, but if your dog's playmate takes offense to that particular game, there could be trouble. You should intervene at the first inkling of dissension. You can't change the style of your dog's play, but you can allow him to play only with dogs who display similar play behavior.

Separation Anxiety

An APBT who cries, howls, or incessantly barks when you leave the house is vocalizing his displeasure at being left alone. Separation anxiety can also be manifested in destructive behavior, like urinating on your bed or chewing furniture legs. This is why crate training is so important. Your APBT must learn that he is in a safe, comfortable place where he will be fine for a while on his own and where he can't do damage to anything or hurt himself.

It is hard not to feel compassion when someone who loves being with you so much is heartbroken in your absence. After all, you can't reassure him that you'll be back soon. But it is best that you don't give in, or you'll end up with an overly dependent dog who becomes a clinging vine even when you *are* home.

Solution

One way to deal with separation anxiety is to keep your comings and goings low-key. Don't bid your APBT goodbye in a sad voice or drag out the departure. When you return, don't lavish hugs and kisses as if you haven't seen each other for months. This is the attention he cries for when you are gone.

Distract your dog from focusing on your departure. Give him a treat or put some peanut butter inside an appropriate toy. You can also leave the radio on softly, because the sound of human voices can be comforting.

Accustom your APBT to staying home alone by leaving him for short periods. Start with a five-minute walk around the block, and gradually build up to half-hour increments. In this way, he will become used to the separations.

You are not at home to observe how your APBT behaves when separation anxiety strikes, but you can videotape him. This can be a particularly helpful evaluation tool if he is left alone uncrated. Place a video recorder on a shelf or counter out of the dog's reach, aimed at an area where he is likely to be. You will then be able to see just what he does after you have left the house. If your dog is crated, as he should be, but barks and cries at your departure, the videotape will give you an idea of the time it takes him to quiet down. It will relieve your own anxiety to see how quickly he settles down once you've actually departed. If anxious behavior persists after six months of diligent conditioning, consult your vet. He may refer you to a behavior specialist or recommend further conditioning.

Separation anxiety in dogs rises commensurately with the number of pet owners who spend the better part of the day away from home. The APBT is a dog who thrives on being with his humans. If you are considering adding him to your family, consider very carefully if your lifestyle will afford him the interaction he needs.

Problem behaviors are the leading cause of pet abandonment, but luckily, some basic training can help to prevent and control many of them. You owe it to your canine family member to make the same effort to resolve his behavioral issues as you

If separation anxiety persists, consult a behavior specialist.

would with any other family member.

We cannot expect APBTs to think like us, but we can try to think like dogs and see things from their point of view. What we see as undesirable behavior may be perfectly normal behavior for a dog. Sorting out the merely distasteful from the potentially dangerous is the first step toward understanding and modifying dog behaviors.

7

ADVANCED TRAINING and ACTIVITIES

With Your American Pit Bull Terrier

Training an APBT goes way beyond shaping a well-behaved pet. It forms a bond between you and your APBT, a relationship built on mutual trust, affection, and respect, qualities that serve you well when carried over into organized activities. Fortunately, the versatility and good-natured temperament of the APBT makes for a wide variety of activities available to you.

THE CANINE GOOD CITIZEN® PROGRAM

Established in 1989 by the AKC, the Canine Good Citizen (CGC) program stresses responsible pet ownership and the importance of being a well-mannered dog. Even though the AKC does not recognize the APBT, all breeds are eligible for the CGC title. Many APBT owners choose the CGC program as the first step in training their dogs, because it lays an excellent foundation for other activities, such as therapy dog programs, law enforcement, agility competition, and more. Successful Canine Good Citizens are included in the AKC's database of CGC-certified dogs, and their owners receive a certificate of accomplishment.

This program is popular with some 4-H Clubs around the country that use CGC as a beginning dog-training course for children. The canine program has been so successful in the United States that other countries are realizing its value as a tool for evaluating a dog's potential.

The CGC test consists of ten sections, each involving regular, everyday occurrences that a normal, well-behaved dog should have no trouble passing:

1. Allowing a friendly stranger to approach.
2. Sitting calmly and politely to be petted.
3. Permitting handling for grooming and physical examination.
4. Heeling on a loose lead.
5. Walking calmly through crowded areas.
6. Sitting on command; downing on command.
7. Coming when called.
8. Greeting another obedient dog without aggression or excitement.
9. Coping with distractions and distracting environments.
10. Behaving well while under the care of another, with the owner out of sight.

Did You Know?

Petting a dog can lower blood pressure and reduce stress.

While these actions are performed during testing, owners are allowed to praise and encourage their APBTs, but the enticement of toys and treats is forbidden. Also prohibited are special training collars such as prong collars, head halters, and electronic collars. Grounds for failure include aggressive behavior by the dog, elimination or marking of territory, and whining or any displays of nervousness.

THERAPY WORK

No one knows better than APBT owners that having a pet is therapeutic. It has been scientifically proven that petting a dog can lower blood pressure and reduce stress. When we're not feeling quite right, our APBTs know that a hug and a few kisses are sometimes the best medicine. Therefore, a fitting occupation for an APBT Canine Good Citizen is work as a therapy dog.

The APBT's love of humans makes him a good choice to provide the curative value of dogs to those who are suffering from pain and loneliness. Therapy dogs visit hospitals and nursing homes, interacting with patients and sharing the love. As a bonus, an APBT in the role of therapy dog goes a long way toward dissolving the myth of the breed's perceived viciousness.

So, how do you help your APBT become a canine therapist? First, you need to learn what organizations in your area provide therapy-dog services. An Internet search will turn up many useful sites to start you off. You can also ask your veterinarian or breeder for information on local therapy-dog programs. Failing all else, call a local assisted-living facility or nursing

If your APBT is well trained and loves people, he may be a good candidate for therapy work.

home and ask if they use such a service, and if so, which one. Pet therapy services usually require participating dogs to complete an in-house training program, sometimes in addition to the Canine Good Citizen certification. This should be a snap for your well-trained APBT, and you'll both feel good about how much you're giving back to the community.

CONFORMATION

Conformation, or showing, is a competition in which a judge evaluates each entrant against the published breed standard. Although not a sport in the strictest sense of the word, conformation nonetheless calls for exacting requirements to be met. Think of it as a Miss America pageant without the talent competition.

Just because the AKC does not acknowledge the APBT does not mean that owners must forego the fun of showing—and showing off—their beautiful dogs. The United Kennel Club (UKC) sponsors conformation activities all over the country that

What to Wear When Showing

You and your dog are a team in the show ring, so it is important that both of you are well groomed and professionally attired. Here are some do's and don'ts:

- DO dress as though you were going to an important job interview.
- DO wear comfortable shoes with good traction that complement your clothing. Leave the spike heels at home.
- DO wear skirts or dresses that allow for freedom of movement and discreet coverage. Pants for women are acceptable, but they should be part of a suit.
- DON'T wear anything with a dog club logo, name, or other personal identification.
- DON'T wear colors that clash with your dog. If your APBT has a very red nose, don't wear a vibrant purple outfit. If you have a dark dog, wear something light to contrast, so that he stands out. Avoid busy prints and patterns.
- DON'T wear blue jeans for any reason.
- DON'T wear anything that will draw attention away from your APBT. He is the real star of the show!

showcase the strength and beauty of the breed. APBTs in conformation trials are judged against the breed standard; the winner is the dog who most closely resembles that standard. Regional conformation shows award champion titles to their winners, who go on to compete against other winning APBTs for the coveted title of Grand Champion.

How do you know if your APBT is competition material? Attend a few local shows and talk to some of the owners and handlers. See how your dog measures up to the veteran APBTs. If you think your dog is a good candidate, do further research. Perhaps a conformation class is available in your area that will teach you the basics of showing.

Keep in mind that a variance in type exists within the APBT breed. A dog who is perfect for the show ring may not be the best candidate for agility competition. Working-form or game-bred APBTs tend to be smallish and more terrier-like. Their temperaments live up to their reputation of being dog aggressive but very people friendly. Show-form APBTs tend to be larger dogs with more expansive chests and bigger heads. Their temperaments tend to be less dog aggressive than their working-form counterparts.

UKC Versus AKC Shows

Because APBTs are not recognized by the AKC, all shows you'll participate in will be sponsored by the UKC or ADBA.

This is unfamiliar territory for the casual dog show fan. Most of the dog shows that are televised are sponsored by the AKC, and the rules are quite different. Obtain a set of the UKC rules and familiarize yourself with them before you venture into the show ring. Unfortunately, ignorance of the law is no excuse; the last thing a judge wants to do is excuse a dog exhibitor for noncompliance.

The first major difference between the two organizations is that most AKC-sponsored shows are all-breed, meaning that all dogs competing in that show are of the same breed, whereas UKC shows are multi-breed, meaning that several different breeds may be participating in one show. In the latter case, the dog club hosting the show can choose which breeds will participate. UKC rules do not allow grooming in the show ring, and the use of food or toys as bait is strictly up to the judge. If she decides to prohibit bait use, anyone with bait in the ring will be excused. Additionally, most UKC events allow last-minute entries on the day of the show, which the AKC does not allow.

The UKC promotes breeder/owner handling; therefore, they do not allow professional dog handlers at conformation events. The shows themselves tend to be smaller and less formal than

In conformation showing, a judge evaluates each entrant against the published breed standard.

AKC events. Unlike their AKC counterparts, UKC judges are encouraged to give the reasons for their placements to the exhibitors. The top prize, Best in Show, is judged by a panel of three, rather than a single judge.

Begin at the Beginning

You've decided that not only do you want to add an APBT to your family, but you want to go into show business. Now you need to find a reputable breeder who can help you select a show-quality puppy.

Most breeders participate in dog shows themselves, so not only will their brood dogs be show quality, but they can give you a lot of the basic information a novice needs. Once you find a breeder you trust, she will help you select from the show-worthy puppies in the litter. Experienced, knowledgeable breeders can evaluate a young puppy and predict whether or not he will grow into a contender.

First, make sure both parents of the litter you choose from have been fully evaluated for all health, temperament, and conformation standards. Without these certifications, you are dealing with a "backyard breeder," no matter how honorable her intentions are. You may have to travel out of state to find a good kennel, and a show-quality dog will cost quite a bit more than a puppy who is pet quality.

What Happens at an APBT Show?

Now that you have selected your puppy and registered him with the UKC and/or ADBA, you are on your way. However, do not expect instant stardom—every rookie has to learn the ropes.

You may feel a bit lost at your first competition, but the relaxed environment of APBT shows will help ease the anxiety. Talk to other handlers; you'll find that everyone's been in the same position before. Other first-timers are probably at the same show as well. Introduce yourself to the judge and explain that you're a beginner. He'll probably give you explanations along the way and second chances to get things right, if time permits.

In the show ring, the judge will look for five major features in your dog, and you need to train him early how to do them:

1. **Be social.** A show dog must be friendly around others. As we've said so many times before, this is even more

Steps to Selecting a Show-Quality Puppy

Adhering to the following steps will help you select a show-quality puppy:

1. Find a breeder you trust; she will be able to help you select a show-quality puppy.
2. Make sure both parents of the litter have been fully evaluated for all health, temperament, and conformation standards.
3. Realize that you may have to travel out of state to find a good kennel.

In the show ring, an APBT must be trained to allow the judge to examine his teeth.

important with APBTs. It would not do for him to act inappropriately at a show where throngs of people are watching. Socialize, socialize, socialize!

2. **Stack correctly.** Stacking refers to the specific position dogs strike when being evaluated by a judge. It is a regal stance that shows off the APBT's attributes while allowing the judge to examine his skeletal and muscular characteristics. His official evaluation of the dog begins with an overview, so your APBT should be at his stacked best!

3. **Politely show teeth.** The "once-over" evaluation includes showing the judge your dog's teeth. Training him to show his bite can be a challenge, because most dogs don't want anyone touching their mouths. This training is very important, for obvious reasons, but it's crucial that the dog be comfortable with being touched and handled all over.

4. **Stand for evaluation.** The APBT must stand still in a stacked position for the judge's overall evaluation. This means no flinching or avoiding the judge's hands.

5. **Gait correctly.** Gaiting refers to the act of demonstrating your dog's movement to the judge at a trot, which is somewhere between a walk and a run. Your APBT will be judged for soundness, smoothness, and the efficiency with which his separate parts work together. The dog should

move fluidly and easily.

The judge will look at the moving dog from three different vantage points: from the side, going directly away from him, and coming right toward him. The handler will always have the dog on her left side, holding the lead in her left hand, and she will always keep the dog between the judge and herself.

Beginners should not expect to win at first. Remember to be a good sport. Congratulate the winners and thank the judges, even though someone else won. After all, by entering your APBT into a dog show, you

Titles and What They Mean

What are all those initials strung after an APBT's registered name? Here is a handy guide to the UKC- and ADBA-awarded titles and what they stand for:

Conformation
CH: Champion
GRCH: Grand Champion

Obedience
CGC: Canine Good Citizen (AKC sponsored, but APBTs are eligible)
U-CD: Companion Dog
U-CDX: Companion Dog Excellent
U-UD: Utility Dog

Weight Pulling
ACE: 100 points achieved in weight-pulling events
ACE OF ACE: Awarded to top weight pullers

Schutzhund
SchH I, II, III: Schutzhund Levels One-Three

Flyball
FD: Flyball Dog
FDX: Flyball Dog Excellent
FDCH: Flyball Dog Champion
FM: Flyball Master
FMX: Flyball Master Champion
FGDCh: Flyball Grand Champion

are essentially asking for the judge's opinion. Be professional, and you will be treated professionally.

Above all, remember that you are at the dog show to have fun, make new friends, and show the world what a beautiful dog the APBT is—especially yours!

OBEDIENCE

Want bragging rights to your APBT's obedience skills? Working or obedience competitions might be your calling. What better activity for a hard-working, eager-to-please breed? You can choose competitions in which you and your APBT perform as a team, or stick to competitions where your dog is the star performer.

As the name implies, obedience competitions are showcases for the owner/handler's training ability and the intelligent APBT's willingness to perform on command. The UKC offers several levels of obedience achievement, and you can garner a string of title abbreviations after your APBT's registered name. A good place to start is the title of Canine Good Citizen (CGH), the only AKC-sponsored title in which APBTs are eligible to participate. You can work your way up the UKC title ladder to Companion Dog (U-CD), Companion Dog Excellent (U-CDX), and Utility Dog (U-UD).

Competitive obedience trials are more involved than showing off how Rover plays dead. Before you begin serious training for competition, get a copy of the UKC's (or in the case of Canine Good Citizen competition, the AKC's) rules and regulations. Attend a few local shows, and observe the dogs performing. See if you can determine what the winners do differently from the dogs who didn't win.

Most obedience titles are awarded after earning three qualifying scores (legs) in the appropriate class under three different judges. Obedience classes offer a perfect score of 200, which is quite rare. Each class exercise has its own point value. A leg is earned after receiving a score of at least 170 total points and at least 50 percent of the points available in each exercise.

After achieving the UD title, you can go on to UDX (Utility Dog Excellent) or OTCh. (Obedience Trial Champion) titles, which are not easy to earn. The UDX title requires you to qualify ten times simultaneously in Open B and Utility B but not necessarily at consecutive shows. The OTCh. title requires a UD holder to earn 100 championship points, a first place in Utility, a first place in Open, and another first place in either class. The placements must be won under three different judges at all-breed obedience trials. A dog who earns this title has the status of the abbreviation OTCh. in front of his name rather than after it.

And you thought the APBT was just a pretty face!

COMPETITIVE SPORTS

We've established that the type of advanced training you undergo should match your goals for your APBT. Do you plan to participate in a sport like flyball or Schutzhund? Maybe you want to encourage your APBT's determined disposition by training him as a weight-pulling dog. The possibilities are limitless, and the titles earned will pale next to the fulfilling time you two will have spent together.

What Is Agility?

Agility is a physically demanding sport in which a coordinated and well-trained dog must navigate an obstacle course within a specified time frame.

Agility

Agility competition is a physically demanding sport in which a coordinated, well-trained APBT will attempt to navigate an intricate obstacle course within a certain time. The obstacles might include ramps, tunnels, seesaws, an elevated dog walk, and more. The best athlete having exceptional drive and the fastest time wins the race.

Although APBTs are certainly athletic dogs, they aren't known for their speed over the long course. Herding breeds definitely have the advantage here. APBTs cannot expect to best Border Collies, Shetland Sheep Dogs (Shelties), or Australian Shepherds, but they can participate in agility trials just for the fun of it. You can bet that your APBT will go for his personal best and have a great time doing it.

In addition to the UKC titles of Agility I, II, and III, other agility titles are awarded by organizations such as the United States Dog Agility Association (USDAA), the North American Dog Agility Association (NADAC), and the Agility Association of Canada (AAC). Each level within each organization has different requirements and scoring systems, so a little homework is required. Most information is available on the Internet.

Flyball

If your APBT is crazy for tennis balls, this sport is for you. Flyball competition consists of relay teams of four dogs and their owners who compete against other teams. One dog per team at a time runs down a course, jumping hurdles and triggering a mechanism that spits out a tennis ball. The dog catches the ball and reverses the course. When the first dog completes the course, the next dog from that team takes his turn. The first team to finish wins.

The North American Flyball Association (NAFA) is the leading organization that sponsors flyball events. Winners accumulate points toward titles that begin with Flyball Dog (FD) and advance to Flyball Grand Champion (FGDCh) and beyond. As in agility competition, some breeds are naturally faster and more agile than APBTs. Our APBTs may not win at flyball, but they sure have fun trying!

If your APBT enjoys retrieving things, flying disc might be the perfect sport for him.

Go-to-Ground (GTG)

Go-to-ground (GTG) is an activity that really showcases the

terrier's instinct for ferreting out rodents and other small prey. The dog is released into the GTG course that has been scented with rat urine. At the end of the course, the terrier will be able to see his "quarry," usually some kind of domestic rodents in a cage. The dog can see and smell them but will not be able to break into the cage or otherwise get at them.

The GTG course is a series of tunnels constructed from 1 × 10-foot (0.30 m × 3.05 m) lengths of board on three sides. Buried underground and reinforced with wood braces, the floor of these tunnels is natural earth. The earth floor and the dark interior mimic a tunnel actually dug by a burrowing animal. The number of right-angle turns corresponds to the level of expertise at which the dog is competing.

Three AKC-sanctioned titles can be earned in GTG: Junior Earthdog (JE), Senior Earthdog (SE), and Master Earthdog (ME). Only AKC-registered breeds may compete for these specific titles, although unofficial GTG competitions are held in which APBTs may participate. Keep in mind that, although the APBT belongs to the terrier group, his go-to-ground instincts have long since been thinned out through breeding. A modern-day APBT does not have the agility to compete against Jack Russells or Rat Terriers. GTG is fun and something that comes very naturally to smaller terriers, but there are more appropriate activities for the APBT. It is better to let him do what he does best: outmuscle and outlast any challenge or obstacle that comes his way.

Flying Disc

Why play with a flying disc with anyone else when your APBT makes the perfect partner? Flying disc is a full-fledged activity that is growing all the time. The discs themselves come in a variety of sizes and materials, soft and hard.

Specialized techniques are available for training your APBT to play with a flying disc that will allow you to start teaching him the game when he is a puppy. Read up on these techniques to avoid accidental injury to the dog. United Frisbee Dog Operations (UFO), which sponsors local, national, and world cup tournaments each year, provides scads of information on training and competing.

Flying disc is a high-energy competitive sport.

Schutzhund

Schutzhund is German for "protection dog." Perhaps the most popular sport for APBTs, Schutzhund focuses on developing protective traits and testing a dog's ability to follow directions. Schutzhund resembles agility and obedience trials but differs in its focus on protection abilities. Originally developed to test the mettle of German Shepherds (hence the name), APBTs are a natural at this sport.

Schutzhund measures a dog's mental stability, stamina, tracking ability, gameness, structural efficiency, and trainability. It also includes a test in which the dog attacks the owner/handler's arm sheathed in a protective burlap sleeve. This should not be misconstrued as an activity that fosters aggression; rather, it's another means of demonstrating

Sports and Safety

Many of the same common-sense guidelines for human athletes apply to APBTs:

- Before starting any activity, ask your vet to check that your APBT is in good health and capable of handling the physical challenges of your chosen sport.
- Pre-event conditioning is a must. Injuries can sideline a dog who does not keep in shape between events.
- Warm-up your APBT before any activity. You never want to take him out of his crate and put him directly in the agility ring or weight pull. Take a brisk walk, toss a ball for a few minutes—anything to get him going.
- Make sure that you properly hydrate your dog. Many dogs won't bother to drink when excited, so give your APBT plenty of water the day before the event. Bring water from home, so that he won't be turned off by "strange" water at the event. If he's very hot, though, avoid ice or ice water, because they can cause cramps. Offer him water right after exercise, and limit him to what he can drink in one minute. Cool him down with easy walking, and then offer a little more water.
- Make sure that the necessary equipment fits your dog. Weight-pull harnesses come in a variety of makes and models; ask other APBT owners which ones they recommend. Check your dog for any signs of skin irritation from the harness after he has competed. The same holds true for leads and collars.

obedience and utility. The Schutzhund dog is trained not to bite anything but the burlap sheath. In fact, frequent mouthing of the burlap sleeves becomes a teeth-cleaning action.

Schutzhund titles are simply SchH I, II, and III, and the levels carry certain age and temperament requirements. At the "master's" level III, tests are geared toward protection of the owner/handler, as well as difficult scent-tracking tests. It is no wonder that many law enforcement personnel and their dogs are attracted to the sport. With proper training and responsibility, Schutzhund is a great family pastime for APBTs and their humans.

Tracking

UKC-sponsored tracking events test a dog's skill at following a scent. The dog must find articles, retrieve them, and return them to the judges. The APBT is suited to this sport due to his terrier instincts that help him flush out small animals. However, he may not surpass smaller terriers or scenthounds in competition.

Officially part of obedience training, tracking has three titles available: Tracking Dog (TD), Tracking Dog Excellent (TDX), and Variable Surface Tracking (VST). If all three titles are attained, the dog then officially becomes a Champion Tracker (CT), with the title abbreviation preceding his name.

Tracking titles may be earned at any time and do not have to come subsequent to earning other obedience titles.

Weight Pulling

The superior strength of the APBT is best demonstrated in weight-pulling competitions, an activity tailor-made for the APBT. Many breeds participate in this intense sport, so here is the APBT's opportunity to eclipse the herding dogs who outshine him in agility. In addition, the American Dog Breeders Association (ADBA) sponsors a weight-pulling contest just for APBTs.

The IWPA

To promote the specialized sport of weight pulling, the International Weight Pull Association (IWPA) was organized in 1984. Membership currently runs about 300 strong and is open to all dogs of all breeds.

In weight pulling, a padded harness is securely fastened to the dog and hitched to carts or vehicles loaded with specific poundage. The competition lies in which dog, within his own weight class, can pull the most weight 16 feet (4.9 m) within one minute. There are eight weight classes and three certificate levels awarded on a point basis. At the end of the season, top point earners in each weight class compete across regions. Not surprisingly, intense conditioning and training are required.

Casual observers might question the "fun factor" of a relatively small dog pulling hundreds of pounds (kilograms). They don't realize that APBTs enjoy the challenge and opportunity to show off their unusual strength. Because the handler/owner is not allowed to have physical contact with the dog during the pull, the decision to compete is strictly up to the canine contestants. They wouldn't bother pulling if they didn't want to!

FUN AND GAMES WITH YOUR APBT

If organized activities don't fit in with your lifestyle, there are still many noncompetitive pastimes to enjoy together with your APBT that will keep his mind and body happily occupied. A dog thrives when he feels his life has purpose; he wants to know that he is a valued family member with something to

Participating in activities with your APBT will help you bond with each other.

contribute. His high energy level requires some sort of outlet, and you want to ensure that it is channeled in a positive way. A bored APBT is a mischievous APBT, so go out and play!

Walking and Jogging

Walking is so much a part of dog ownership that it hardly seems worthy of special mention, yet it is the easiest and one of the most beneficial things that you can do—for both of you.

What constitutes a quality walk with a healthy adult APBT? Owner and dog should walk briskly together on a hard surface for approximately 3 miles (4.8 km). A hard surface like concrete adds the bonus of grooming your APBT while you're both getting exercise, because it will wear down his nails like a file. In fact, a sure sign that your dog isn't being walked enough is when you have to trim his nails yourself. Walk a minimum of 3 miles (4.8 km) at least four times a week, and you may never again need those nail clippers.

Weather influences the frequency and length of your walks. On very hot days, it is best to stay inside with the air conditioning and save the walk for cooler temperatures. In cold weather, a brisk walk will keep him warm, with the emphasis on *brisk*. A dog's normal pace is faster than yours; if you slow him down by walking at a human's normal pace, he won't be getting much of a workout. A fast walk or easy jog will pace you more evenly with your APBT.

Camping

Imagine how much fun an APBT could have camping. Why, it's like a walk that never ends! It gives dog and owner yet another way to bond, and it gives you the extra security of having your dog with you.

Before you air out the sleeping bags, you'll need to check on a few things to make your trip as safe and enjoyable as possible. Find out if the campgrounds allow dogs, and if so, see if they are also allowed on trails. Unfortunately, irresponsible dog owners have abused the privilege of camping with their dogs by breaking campground rules, and now many campgrounds do not permit dogs. You can help turn the tide by diligently cleaning up after your APBT, keeping him from disturbing other campers, and obeying all rules.

You'll want to assess your APBT's experience with the great outdoors. No doubt he's had enough regular exercise that his paw pads are toughened and general fitness level is good. Remember that camping will expose him to all kinds of parasites. You may wish to consider a vaccine against Lyme disease and some kind of flea/tick repellant.

Dogs are not so very different from humans in that, without enjoyable physical activity, they can become depressed, out of shape, and lethargic. Finding an activity that you both enjoy isn't all that hard; you just have to think outside the box a little. You don't have to become an expert in Schutzhund to fulfill your APBT's athletic needs, when brisk daily walks do very well in maintaining his physical fitness. The bottom line is that your APBT doesn't care what activity he's doing, as long as he gets to do it with his favorite person: you.

HEALTH

of Your American Pit Bull Terrier

Every dog owner wants a healthy pet, but problems are bound to arise from time to time. Your APBT's good health depends on more than preventive veterinary medicine. He can't tell you in words if he's feeling sick or where something hurts, so it's up to you to gain a working knowledge of canine health and fitness. Become familiar with the everyday canine ailments, as well as any specific physical conditions APBTs are prone to contracting. Learn to interpret your dog's behavior and body language to identify possible health issues and what action to take, and work as a team with your vet to provide the best health care possible at the animal hospital and at home.

FINDING A VETERINARIAN

Hale and hearty, with a high tolerance for pain, your APBT will rarely show signs of illness. If he does, though, he is probably in enough pain to be unable to keep up a pretense of good health, so of course you must take him to the vet right away. But how do you find a reliable veterinarian in the first place?

Advance Preparation

One of the first things you will do when adding a dog to your family is to get him a medical checkup. This means that your quest for a reputable vet will begin *before* you bring home a new puppy or adult APBT. You'll want to continue the health maintenance regime started by his breeder or original owner, so if a new puppy's breeder is local, ask for a reference. You're not obligated to continue using the same veterinarian your breeder does, but there are advantages to doing so. Your APBT's medical record will already have been established, and the doctor will be familiar with the dog.

Talk to other dog owners in your neighborhood, and find out what animal hospital they use. If you know of other APBT owners, ask them who they recommend. The ideal vet will have hands-on experience with the breed. Contact the American Animal Hospital Association (AAHA) for a list of affiliated veterinarians in your area.

The First Checkup

A nursing puppy receives protective antibodies from his mother's milk, but this natural immunity wanes with time. When a puppy is around 8 to 10 weeks old—coincidentally, the same time many puppies leave their breeders for new homes— he becomes susceptible to a number of illnesses. That is why it is so important to take him for a veterinary checkup as soon as possible, ideally within 24 hours. Your APBT puppy will already have received his first vaccinations and wormings, but do not skip this checkup, even if you use the same veterinarian the breeder used. Certain skin disorders and external parasites prey on puppies, and the vet will assess the pup's general condition

Annual booster shots throughout your dog's lifetime will help him remain healthy.

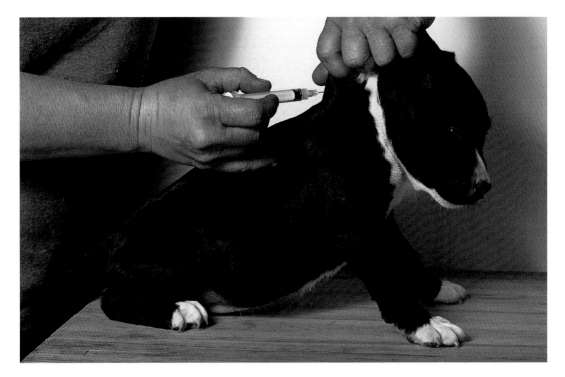

and point out any problems. She will also take this opportunity to discuss future vaccinations and heartworm prevention.

The vet will check your puppy's vital signs and body temperature. A normal body temperature for dogs is higher than for humans, around 101°F (38.3°C) or 102°F (38.9°C). The vet will also examine the puppy's coat, and his ears will be checked for signs of allergy or infection. She will examine the eyes for growths, abnormal secretions, or early cataract formation. A stethoscope will detect any heart or lung abnormalities that may require further testing. In addition, the vet will palpate the abdomen for tumors or bladder stones. She'll also look inside the mouth for tissue or tooth problems. Lastly, she will examine the puppy's feet. Paw pads are still pink and tender at this age, so the vet will check for any punctures or cuts and trim long nails. Once your new puppy is declared sound, you can take him home and enjoy each other.

The Vaccination Controversy

Currently, controversy exists regarding vaccinating dogs against canine illnesses. Some owners believe that introducing toxins into the body does more harm than good, while other owners believe their pts don't have enough contact with the outside world to subject them to certain diseases. Overall, it is generally safe to say that APBTs do benefit from vaccinations.

VACCINATIONS

Canine health care has long included vaccinations against deadly diseases like rabies. Rabies vaccines are even required by law. If a person is bitten by a dog who does not have proof of rabies vaccination, the victim is considered at risk for the disease. A dog in the early stages of rabies may be asymptomatic, so the only way to learn if he has the disease is by posthumous testing. In short, a rabies vaccine can save your dog's life.

Rabies aside, some controversy exists over the benefits of vaccinating your dog against canine illnesses. Some owners believe that introducing toxins into the body with these vaccines does more harm than good. Other dog owners believe that their pets don't have enough contact with the outside world to subject them to certain diseases.

Assuming that responsible owners know that APBTs will spend a good amount of time indoors and outdoors, it is fair to say that APBTs benefit from vaccinations. Combination shots like the DHLPP reduce the number of separate vaccinations the dog will endure. With the DHLPP, a single injection protects against distemper, hepatitis, leptospirosis, parvovirus, and parainfluenza (kennel cough). Annual booster shots throughout the dog's lifetime will give him an edge on good health and give you peace of mind.

Dogs are commonly vaccinated against some or all of the following diseases.

Distemper

Distemper is the number-one killer of unvaccinated dogs. It is easily passed from one dog to another and usually attacks puppies, although older dogs may get it, too. It can be difficult to diagnose, even for a seasoned veterinarian.

Symptoms of distemper vary and include vomiting, diarrhea, cough, lack of appetite, fever, nasal discharge, inflamed eyes, and lethargy. Treatment at the first suspicion of distemper greatly increases a pup's chances for survival. Dogs with full-blown distemper occasionally survive, although often with permanent brain or nervous system damage.

Treatment for distemper depends on the stage of infection. Your dog may receive anticonvulsants, antibiotics to prevent secondary bacterial infection, eye ointment, medication to stop diarrhea and vomiting, or fluids that your vet may administer to counteract dehydration.

Did You Know?

Distemper is the number-one killer of unvaccinated dogs.

Canine Bordetellosis

Also known as *bordetella* or *kennel cough*, canine bordetellosis is caused by a bacterium present in the respiratory tracts of many animals. Symptoms resemble a bad cold and include a runny nose and a hacking cough. In otherwise healthy adult dogs, the illness usually runs its course in a few days, but it can be life-threatening to a puppy or senior dog. Treatment includes isolating the dog to prevent the spread of infection and resting in a humid environment. Run a vaporizer or humidifier in his sleeping area, and encourage him to nap there. With your vet's approval, administer a mild children's cough syrup to help soothe his cough, which in turn will save him energy. The illness should run its course in two weeks.

Bordetella awareness first arose when dogs began returning home from boarding kennels with terrible coughs. Because transmission occurs through contact with the nasal secretions of infected dogs, kennels were the perfect breeding ground. Fortunately, the illness is not serious, but boarding facilities now require their canine guests to be vaccinated against it. The vaccine usually consists of a quick nasal spray, but it is also available via injection. If your APBT has contact with other dogs on a regular basis or is going to be boarded, consult with your vet to establish a vaccination schedule and method that is best for your dog.

Infectious Canine Hepatitis

Infectious hepatitis in dogs affects the liver, just as it does in humans, although dogs cannot transmit it to humans. It is spread from one dog to another via contact with infected urine, stool, or saliva.

Symptoms of hepatitis are

If your APBT appears to be unusually lethargic and has no appetite, consult your vet.

similar to those for distemper and include vomiting, diarrhea, cough, lack of appetite, fever, nasal discharge, inflamed eyes, and lethargy, with the additional symptom of intense thirst.

Treatment depends on the severity of the illness, with acute cases requiring hospitalization. Your vet will administer antibiotics to prevent further bacterial complications, vitamin supplements, and nondairy fluids to soothe an inflamed throat. During recovery, the dog should have plenty of fresh water, and upon the advice of your veterinarian, eat several small fat-free meals throughout the day. Early detection is crucial to your dog's survival, because the disease spreads rapidly and is often fatal.

Leptospirosis

Leptospirosis is caused by a spirochete, a microorganism often carried by rats. An unvaccinated dog risks infection if he has contact with a rat or eats something contaminated by a rat.

Symptoms of leptospirosis include bloody stool or urine, fever, depression, red eyes and mouth, painful mouth sores, vomiting, thirst, lack of appetite, and pain when moving.

Quick medical treatment for leptospirosis is necessary, not

only because it can permanently damage the kidneys or liver, but because it is transmissible to humans. Treatment is usually streptomycin, an antibiotic. Acute cases may need hospitalization, but most can recover at home. Your vet will explain the proper precautions owners must take to protect themselves when caring for an afflicted APBT.

Parvovirus

Parvovirus is a deadly disease unheard of in dogs until 1977, when experts believe a strain of feline distemper virus mutated to infect canines. The virus is easily spread through contaminated stool that ends up on paws or shoes.

Early symptoms of parvovirus are depression and appetite loss, followed by vomiting, diarrhea, and fever. This killer spreads rapidly, attacking the stomach lining, bone marrow, lymph nodes, and in young puppies, the heart (myocardial parvovirus). Puppies with infected hearts can die suddenly or within a few days of contracting the illness. The few who survive may develop chronic heart problems later in life.

Treatment depends on the symptoms, the severity of the disease, and the dog's age. Hospitalization is usually necessary. Your dog will probably receive medications to stop vomiting and diarrhea, antibiotics to kill any secondary bacterial infections, and fluids to counteract dehydration.

The Truth About Rabies Transmission

Rabies is a virus-borne diseases that can be transmitted by a variety of wild animals. Highly contagious, the disease is passed through infected saliva to other animals and humans through bites, open cuts, or scratches.

Parainfluenza

Parainfluenza is not an overtly dangerous disease. Several different viruses, as well as a bacterium, cause the illness that spreads so easily among dogs. Because of the frequent hacking cough that develops when infected, and because boarding kennels are common places to contract the disease, parainfluenza is commonly referred to as "kennel cough," although the term is more correctly applied to bordetella. Dogs who spend any time in commercial boarding kennels are required to be inoculated against kennel cough, although even vaccinated dogs sometimes contract the disease. Symptoms are not debilitating, and some afflicted dogs don't even miss a meal. Parainfluenza usually runs its course, but your vet may prescribe antibiotics to prevent complications and medicine to ease coughing.

Rabies

Perhaps more than any other animal disease, rabies has been hyped everywhere, from literature to urban legend. It has always been known to be a guaranteed killer of humans and canines, although the first human to survive untreated rabies was recently documented. This virus-borne disease is not limited to dogs and can be transmitted by all manner of wild animals. One reason it is so highly contagious is that infected saliva can pass the virus to other animals and humans. Infectious saliva is most commonly transmitted through bites, but it can also infect a person or animal by coming into contact with open cuts or scratches.

Rabies affects the nervous system, and one of the first symptoms is a change in disposition. A gentle dog may become aggressive (think Cujo), or an independent dog may become clingy. Soon, the dog's pupils will dilate, and bright light will bother him. He will become aloof and show signs of stomach upset and fever. As the disease worsens, he may demonstrate poor coordination, facial tics, random biting, and a loss of control of facial muscles, resulting in an open, drooling mouth. In the final stages, the dog will lapse into a coma and die. No effective treatment for canine rabies exists.

All warm-blooded animals are potential victims of rabies, so it is easy to see why vaccination is required. With simple preventive medicine, we can protect all our loved ones from this dreadful disease.

Coronavirus

Sometimes called "corona," canine coronavirus is a viral infection of a dog's intestinal lining. There are different strains of coronavirus that can infect many species of animals and birds, including humans, but canine coronavirus does not affect humans. Severe acute respiratory syndrome (SARS) is a type of coronavirus.

A dog afflicted with coronavirus transmits the disease organism through feces. Other dogs catch it through contaminated food bowls or by direct contact with the sick dog. Symptoms include lethargy, decreased appetite, and sudden diarrhea that is orange tinted, foul smelling, and may contain blood. The symptoms are easily confused with parvovirus, so see the vet promptly.

No cure is available for coronavirus, and it usually runs its course in several days, but treatment is still necessary. Dehydration from the severe diarrhea may require intravenous fluids. In addition, secondary bacterial infections are common, so your vet may prescribe antibiotics.

Lyme Disease

Caused by a bacterium, Lyme disease spreads to dogs and humans alike through the bite of an infected tick, usually the deer tick. Deer tick nymphs are so tiny (about the size of a poppy seed) that they are easily overlooked. Most infected people are not even aware that they have been bitten. Only when severe joint pain, fatigue, fever, and/or skin rash send them to the doctor do they discover that they have been infected.

Lyme disease has been found on every continent except Antarctica, and it is particularly prevalent in the eastern United States. The symptoms appear about two months after infection, and treatment typically includes antibiotics and analgesics (pain relievers). Recovery time varies according to the severity of the case and how early it was detected.

A Lyme disease vaccine is available for dogs, but it is not always necessary. Your vet can help you decide if your APBT would benefit from the vaccine.

SHOULD YOU BREED YOUR APBT?

The idea of a whole basketful of cuddly puppies is so appealing that you might be tempted to breed your APBT. You might also think that your APBT is the handsomest ever, and you want to share the wealth. As with many ideals, reality often comes like a bucket of cold water, and you don't want to find yourself drenched and dripping all over the whelping box.

The decision to breed your dog is one that must be carefully considered and thoroughly researched before taking action, especially with the APBT. As you already know, indiscriminate breeding only furthers the APBT's infamous reputation. On the other hand, responsible breeding can help educate the public on the truths behind the myths.

Compelling arguments exist for and against dog breeding. Study them all, and then make an intelligent decision that is best for you and your APBT.

The decision to breed your APBT is not one that should be undertaken lightly.

Advantages and Disadvantages of Breeding

Many things must be considered when thinking about breeding your dog and even more when thinking about breeding an APBT. Contrary to popular belief, breeding a bitch is not a fun, easy way to make money. The hefty price tags on purebred puppies are usually break-even reimbursement for stud fees, prenatal health care, and delivery and postdelivery necessities. A responsible breeder breeds her dog because she is concerned for the future of APBTs and wants it to continue. Far too many people breed their dogs without seeing the big picture, and the dogs and puppies suffer the consequences.

There are many reasons *not* to breed your APBT and only one really good reason to breed: a true love of the breed itself. Careful breeding uses science and thorough pedigree research to increase the chances of puppies inheriting desirable traits. Every happy, healthy APBT who enters the world and is placed in a responsible home is another testament to society that the breed is not innately menacing. It is gratifying to know that you have personally contributed to that goal.

When shouldn't you breed your APBT? Any time that you ask yourself what motivates your desire and the answer is anything other than the reason just given. Rationalizing that females are happier when bred, or that you want your children to experience the miracle of birth is unacceptable. Remember, you are making decisions that affect the dog's life more than yours. For an APBT bitch, the process of breeding—from mating to birthing—is stressful and taxing. Pregnancies are not always easy. Delivery may endanger the mother's life, and many puppies die during or shortly after whelping. Your life will be impacted, too. Whelping can occur at the most inconvenient moment, and delivery of the entire litter can take a long time. True, dogs in the wild have many litters without human intervention, but a responsible APBT owner knows that someone should stand by to help during the whelping process, especially if serious complications arise. Would you be emotionally, physically, and financially prepared to rush your APBT to an after-hours veterinary clinic for an emergency C-section in the middle of the night?

Nature takes its own course, but a good breeder helps keep it on the straight and narrow.

Neutering (Spaying and Castrating)

Neutering refers to the surgical removal or alteration of certain reproductive organs in dogs. A female is *spayed*, which is the same as having an ovariohysterectomy. Her uterus and ovaries are removed under general anesthesia, rendering her incapable of having puppies. Alternatively, she can undergo a tubal ligation, a process in which the oviducts are cut to prevent any sperm from reaching eggs. Male dogs, on the other hand, are *castrated*, meaning their testicles are surgically removed.

The primary reason that dogs should be neutered is to help with population control. Too many unwanted pets roam the streets, unaltered and free to mate with other strays and produce even more homeless litters. A stray dog who just looks in part like a "pit bull" faces euthanasia if caught by animal control authorities, even if he didn't demonstrate any aggression.

There are other reasons to neuter your pet APBT. Females will not go into heat, which means no mess for you and no barking, marking suitors for her. Also, she won't be interested in breaking away from your home or yard in search of male dogs. Because estrogen is one of the primary causes of canine mammary cancer, a female who has been spayed before she has her first heat will be less apt to develop this common malignant tumor. Ovariohysterectomy also eliminates the possibility of any tumors in the uterus and ovaries. As spayed bitches get older, however, they may develop incontinence issues, seemingly more so than intact aging bitches. Medications often help clear up minor cases of incontinence, but sometimes they have no effect, and doggy diapers are the only recourse.

Castrating your male pet has even more discernible results. The male hormone testosterone is produced in the testicles. By removing them, you eliminate many of the unwanted dog behaviors rooted in the hormone. Increased aggression (toward dogs and people), roaming, and urine marking are all testosterone-induced, which is why castration is favored over vasectomy. A vasectomy, which severs or removes the seminal ducts, thwarts fertilization but does nothing to reduce the undesirable behaviors. Castrated males also make better students and workers, as they are not distracted by the scent of any females in heat. *Pheromones*, the scent stimulus that alerts males to females in season, can travel great distances in the air. A castrated dog will not detect or respond to pheromones, giving him a much longer attention span during training. Medically, castration eliminates the risk of testicular and prostate tumors, reduces the risk of hernias, and halts the inheritance of harmful genetic traits like hip dysplasia and epilepsy.

When should you castrate or spay your dog? In the United States, most dogs are altered between five and eight months of age, although some shelters and veterinarians neuter males as young as six weeks and females as young as two months. Such early procedures may require different anesthetics and closer body temperature monitoring, but they are otherwise safe.

Pet-Quality Puppies

Dog shows are a showcase for breeding stock, so APBTs who will participate in conformation shows cannot be neutered. Breeders typically sell their "pet-quality" puppies to people who just want a loving family pet, and they require that the dog be neutered. This does not mean that these puppies are in any way inferior in health or temperament. Most likely, they have some physical attribute, such as a kinked tail or albinism, that disqualifies them from conformation competition. Breeders do not want these undesirable traits to continue in the bloodline, so they require that these dogs be neutered.

PARASITES

Parasites fall into two groups: external parasites, which live on the outside of your dog's body, and internal parasites, which live inside the body. Both can be the bane of your dog's existence if not treated. They can make him uncomfortable, sick, and downright miserable. In extreme cases, such as when heartworms are involved, they can kill.

As humans have discovered over the last few hundred years, good grooming and clean living conditions help protect against parasites. Modern veterinary medicine also has produced an array of preventive treatments that effectively reduce our dogs' risk of parasite infestation. Discuss with your vet which parasites you should beware of and what treatments are best suited to your dog.

Internal Parasites

In addition to vaccinating against contagious diseases, your vet will perform a yearly check for internal parasites like heartworms and several kinds of intestinal worms. Conscientious breeders see that their litters receive the necessary treatment for intestinal worms, a common affliction of puppies. Many pups are born with roundworms, and those who aren't can easily become infested. A puppy should be worm-free by the time he goes to his new home, but that does not guarantee against future worm infestations.

A dog with intestinal worms will show signs of general malaise: a dry coat, dull eyes, weakness, coughing, vomiting, diarrhea, and weight loss despite a hearty appetite. Some dogs, though, will lose their appetite entirely, and still others will show no symptoms at all until worm infestation makes them severely anemic. Because the symptoms are similar for all kinds of worms, you won't know exactly what he has until the stool is tested.

Tapeworms

A dog becomes infected with tapeworms by eating an intermediate host that contains an immature form of the worm. Fleas ingest tapeworm eggs, which hatch into larvae within the flea. When a dog eats infected fleas, the larvae develop into the adult worms, sometimes growing to be several feet (meters) long. Adult tapeworms feed on the host's digesting food, robbing the host of nutrition. Humans infested with tapeworms are constantly hungry and eat ravenously but don't gain weight. (This is not the next miracle diet trick, so don't try it at home.)

Extreme cases can be fatal.

Dogs infected with tapeworms rarely exhibit symptoms, although you may notice short white worm segments in the stool or in the hair around the anus. These segments are egg sacs that break off the adult worm and resemble wriggling grains of rice. They tickle the anus, and the dog may scoot his behind along the floor to relieve the itching. If you see any worms in his feces, or if he scoots along the floor, take him to the vet. The condition is easily treated with a solution, administered orally or by injection, that dissolves the worms. However, you also need to address the issue of fleas, because they are the most common tapeworm carriers.

Dogs suffering from internal parasites experience weight loss despite a hearty appetite.

Roundworms

Roundworms are very common parasites in puppies and adult dogs. Even puppies from responsible breeders often have them. If the mother dog ever had roundworms, she may have larvae encysted in her body that she can pass on through her milk, even though an examination showed no infestation. Puppies in utero can be infested when the mother's larvae migrate to their lungs during pregnancy. Every puppy in the litter will most likely be born with roundworms and require several treatments. Dogs and humans can also pick up roundworms from the ground, where the eggs have been deposited by other animals, including beetles, earthworms, and rodents.

Roundworms look like

strands of spaghetti and can be up to 8 inches (20.3 cm) long. Like the tapeworm, they feed off the host's digesting food. Infested puppies at first will eat voraciously but will quickly become weak from malnutrition and stop eating altogether. A pup with an acute or chronic roundworm infestation will get a potbelly (noticeably larger than "puppy belly") and suffer from diarrhea and vomiting. The condition is easily treated, but humans in the family who have contact with a puppy suffering from roundworms must be especially vigilant about their own hygiene. If a stool sample confirms that your dog has worms, a variety of effective drugs are available for your vet to prescribe. Over the course of treatment, stool samples will be checked for efficacy.

The Danger of Hookworms

Hookworms can cause severe iron-deficiency anemia in dogs, and they can be problematic for humans, too. They are transmitted through infected feces.

Whipworms

In North America, whipworms are among the most common parasitic worms in dogs. These worms attach themselves to the lower part of the intestine to feed. They can live for months or even years in a dog, spending their larval stage in the small intestine, the adult stage in the large intestine, and passing eggs through the dog's feces. Dogs ingest the eggs or immature worms by eating infected feces, a habit that can be as harmful as it is distasteful.

The affected dog may only have an upset stomach and a little diarrhea, making the parasite difficult to diagnose. The only way to detect whipworms is with an examination of a stool sample, and even this is not infallible. Dogs successfully treated for whipworms are often reinfected from exposure to the eggs deposited on the ground in the feces. Whipworm eggs can survive outside, exposed to the elements, for as long as five years, waiting to infest—or reinfest—a host. This underscores the importance of cleaning up droppings, whether in your own backyard or a public park.

If a stool sample confirms the presence of whipworms, the vet will give your dog a strong deworming agent. Left untreated, anemia can develop.

Hookworms

Dog owners in the United States must be concerned with four different species of this blood-sucking worm, and the most common and most serious species are found in warm climates. One species prefers colder climates, thus posing a concern for dog owners in the northern United States and Canada.

Hookworms can cause severe iron-deficiency anemia in dogs, and they pose a problem for humans, too. (Transmission is through infected feces, but hookworms cannot complete their life cycle in a human host. They simply infest the skin and cause irritation.) Using pooper-scoopers or disposable gloves when cleaning up waste is a good way to prevent hookworm infestation.

In dogs, hookworms attach themselves to the intestines to feed, changing locations about six times a day. Because he loses blood each time the hookworm repositions itself, the dog can become anemic. Symptoms of hookworm infestation include dark stools, weight loss, general weakness, pale skin coloration, and skin that is swollen and red from penetration of the larvae, usually at the feet. Fortunately, a number of proven medications are available to rid the host of these parasites. Most heartworm preventives include a hookworm antihelmintic (antiworm) preparation, as well.

Ringworm

Ringworm is not really a worm but a very contagious fungus that spreads easily among animals and humans through contact with infected skin or hair. Infective spores are constantly dropped off the hair and skin of infected dogs or people, and contact with even one spore is all it takes to catch it. The ringworm fungus feeds on dead surface skin and hair cells, causing an irritating itch. It typically appears on dogs as a raw-looking bald patch that sometimes appears scaly, without the rawness.

In typical fungal fashion, ringworm is difficult to eliminate. It is very hardy in the environment and can live for years. It can be resistant to treatment, which is usually a combination of topical and systemic therapy. Painstaking attention to hygiene and complete decontamination of the dog's environment must be continued until the vet declares the dog ringworm free. Children, adults, and the elderly with compromised immune systems are most susceptible. If your dog is diagnosed with ringworm and you do not have it at that time, chances are you won't catch it.

Heartworms

Heartworms are deadly parasites transmitted from dog to dog through mosquito bites. When a heartworm-infested mosquito bites the dog, it injects larvae into the skin. The larvae then enter the dog's circulatory system and take up residence in the blood vessels. It can be a full eight months after the bite before the worms mature. As they start to interfere with the action of the heart, symptoms appear, such as a chronic cough, weight loss, and fatigue. Heart failure ultimately claims the dog's life.

Is an infestation of adult heartworms treatable? Yes. However, treatment is expensive, long, and risky, although not as dangerous as the heartworms themselves. The process kills the adult heartworms, but dead worms in the heart can provoke a fatal clot in the blood vessels or chambers.

Prevention is a far better way to spare your APBT a premature death from this disease. Your vet can tell you the right age to start your dog on a heartworm preventive, as well as which ones she recommends. A monthly dose of the medicine, usually in the form of a meaty morsel or tasty tablet, is all it takes to guard against heartworms throughout your dog's lifetime. There is a catch, though: Your dog must be tested and found free of heartworms *before* starting a preventive regimen. A dog already harboring heartworms can become critically ill from the same medicine that prevents infestation. Heartworm prevention is not foolproof, and a slight chance always exists that your dog will become infested after taking the preventive. Because the symptoms do not present themselves for many months, you could innocently make your infected dog sick by continuing his heartworm preventive. This is why it is important to have your APBT's blood tested once a year for the presence of heartworms.

External Parasites

Fleas, ticks, and mites all think that your APBT make the perfect host. Unfortunately, these guests only make him uncomfortable and potentially sick. They can be found anywhere on his body but typically settle down on the head and neck.

Parasite prevention often means introducing insecticides into your dog's body, the long-term effects of which concern many dog owners. No documentation suggests that long-term pesticide use poses health risks, but plenty of information is available on parasite-borne diseases. Talk to your vet about the safest and best course of action for the well-being of your APBT.

Ticks

Ticks feed off their host's blood by burrowing their mouths into the skin. More than just a nuisance, ticks can be disease carriers. The tiny deer tick is especially known to be a carrier of Lyme disease, a flu-like illness that causes fatigue, fever, loss of appetite, and swollen neck glands. Humans are susceptible to Lyme disease, so take care that you are not bitten. Ticks are also bearers of Rocky Mountain spotted fever, which can cause paralysis in dogs.

Ticks come in many sizes and colors, from brown to almost blue, and they are pretty easy to spot on the APBT's short coat. Old wives' tales recommend removal by methods such as

Be sure to inspect your APBT for ticks after he has been playing outdoors.

Tick Removal: What Not to Do

- DON'T use a sharp implement.
- DON'T crush, puncture, or squeeze the tick's body.
- DON'T apply substances to the tick (like petroleum jelly, gasoline, lidocaine). These "folk" remedies are supposed to make the tick pull out of the host, but studies show that they don't work.
- DON'T apply a hot match or nail to the tick. The theory is that the tick will be burned and pull out of the host. Even if the method is effective, the risk of burning your dog is too great.
- DON'T pull the tick out with a twisting or jerking action.
- DON'T handle the tick with bare hands.

holding a hot match tip to the tick or piercing it with a needle. The simplest, safest way to remove a tick is to pull it out with a pair of blunt tweezers that you dedicate to the role of tick remover. Grasp the tick as close to its head as possible, pull it out with a steady movement, and flush it down the toilet. Try not to rupture or squeeze the tick's body; you don't want potentially infectious body fluids to get on the dog's skin or your hand. If part of the tick's head remains attached to the dog's skin, apply an antiseptic to the site. The head will eventually fall off.

Mites

Ear mites are nasty little critters that live in the ear canal. They irritate your APBT's sensitive ears and produce a dry, rusty-brown discharge. If you see your dog constantly scratching or pawing at his ears, or notice inflammation or discharge, have your vet check for ear mites.

Mange mites are tiny buggers that can cause big dermatological problems for your APBT. They can cause sarcoptic mange, making his skin itchy and crusty and raising little red bumps.

Follicular mange is caused by a different type of mite and may or may not cause itching. Regardless, you will notice small, bare patches in your dog's fur that give him a moth-eaten look. Medicine from the vet will clear up this condition.

Fleas

Fleas are by far the hardest external parasite to eliminate. Not only do they reproduce incredibly fast, but they can actually adapt to insecticides and become resistant. How do you know if your APBT is bothered by fleas? Separate a patch of his fur to examine his skin. If you see tiny black flecks that look like pepper, that's flea "dirt," or excrement. You will undoubtedly find your dog scratching a lot as well. Some dogs develop serious allergic reactions to flea bites that make them miserable. Prompt veterinary treatment is in order to ease the skin irritations and prevent infection. Your vet will also tell you how to rid the dog and your home of these stubborn pests.

COMMON HEALTH ISSUES IN THE APBT

Some dog breeds and breed groups are more prone to certain health conditions than other breeds. It is widely believed that APBTs as a breed are prone to allergies, cataracts, congenital heart disease, hip dysplasia, and von Willebrand's disease. Actually, no definitive evidence suggests that APBTs are predisposed to specific health problems beyond those that can affect any terrier or any dog. An APBT whose parents have no obvious signs of inherited tendencies like hip dysplasia are unlikely to have specific inherited health issues.

Although APBTs are not known for many breed-specific disorders, they are as much at risk as the next dog for some common diseases that once were death sentences. Fortunately, advances in veterinary medicine give sick dogs second chances that weren't available until quite recently.

Allergies

Allergies have reached epidemic proportions today in animals and humans. Humans sneeze and experience watery eyes when afflicted with an allergy, but dogs with allergies typically get itchy skin that is as bothersome to them as our runny noses are to us.

Allergies can be grouped into four categories: flea, atopic or inhalant, food, and contact.

- **Flea Allergy:** The most common type of allergy is the flea allergy. This isn't an allergy to the flea itself but to a

Fighting Fleas

Follow the steps below to help fight fleas:

- Identify "hot spots," like places where your APBT sleeps. Spray them with a nontoxic flea larvicide.
- Regularly wash your dog's bedding.
- Spray outdoor "hot spots" (such as doghouses, outdoor bedding, and your dog's favorite spots on the lawn) with insecticide. Use vet-recommended products to kill fleas and their eggs on your dog.
- Vacuum every other day to rid carpets of eggs and larvae.

protein in its saliva left in the skin after a flea bite. Severe reactions can make the dog miserable.

• **Inhalant Allergies:** Inhalant allergies are the second most common type of allergy in dogs, and a dog experiences them when he breathes in an offending allergen, whether it is pollen, tobacco smoke, or mold spores. Even if an allergic dog stays indoors all the time, outside allergens will find their way into your house and your dog's nose. Your vet can discuss treatment with you.

• **Food Allergies:** Food allergies in dogs are often caused by the same foods that humans are allergic to: soy, milk, eggs, wheat, corn, and chicken. The most likely reaction is itchy, irritated skin, although vomiting and diarrhea may occur. Food allergies must be isolated by trial and error, but once the culprit is found, it is not hard to customize the dog's diet.

• **Contact Allergies:** With contact allergies, reactions occur when physically touching a substance containing an

Some dogs suffer from contact allergies, which means that a reaction occurs when physically touching a substance containing an allergen, such as grass.

allergen. Contact allergens include plastic, grass, and wool. Allergy shots are often used to cope with the uncomfortable symptoms, and lifestyle changes may be necessary. An APBT who is allergic to his plastic food dish, for example, should switch to a steel or ceramic bowl, but an APBT who is allergic to grass is more of a challenge. The owner must provide an alternate surface for exercise and relaxation, such as an enclosed tennis court to run in or long, brisk walks on asphalt or cement, and a dog bed for the backyard.

Shots and medications such as antihistamines and steroids are good for occasional allergy flare-ups, but for ongoing allergy problems, dog owners should investigate other means, like immunotherapy. Immunotherapy is designed to desensitize the dog to the allergen by building up immunity to it through injections containing small amounts of the allergen itself or extracts of the allergen. A great number of dogs respond well to this treatment alone, although some may need medication in addition to the shots.

Allergies cannot be genetically controlled or predicted, but they can be managed. All it takes is patience and tenacity to identify the problem and the determination to work around it.

Blood Disorders

Blood disorders can be particularly serious because they interfere with the blood's ability to deliver oxygen and nutrients to all the cells of the body. In the case of von Willebrand's disease, the blood's ability to clot properly is also affected.

von Willebrand's Disease

Von Willebrand's disease is a genetic bleeding disorder sometimes seen in APBTs. It is characterized by excessive bleeding, first noticed during procedures like dew claw removals or ear croppings, and it can be life threatening in its most severe form.

Three types of von Willebrand's disease are recognized. Type III, which is the most fatal, is most often seen in Scottish Terriers (Scotties). Type I is the most common, and it is thought to be the predominant type in APBTs afflicted with the disease, although no scientific studies have yet proven this.

Skin Allergies

Skin conditions aren't more of a problem for APBTs than for any other breeds, but the dog's coloration can make a difference. Blue- and white-coated APBTs tend to suffer from skin problems more than their dark counterparts do. Allergies can also contribute to rashes and "hot spots." (Hot spots are superficial bacterial infections on the skin that itch or otherwise cause the animal to lick or chew the area persistently, worsening the condition. The inflamed area can feel warm, look red, and spread quickly.) Skin allergies can be aggravated by certain foods, insect bites, or climate, but diligent coat grooming can help catch skin problems before they become bothersome.

Blood tests can determine the range of genetic tendency toward the disease. Some dogs may be carriers without suffering from the disease itself, so testing of brood dogs is essential. Puppies as young as seven weeks can also be tested for the presence of von Willebrand's disease.

Cancer

Smallpox. Bubonic plague. Polio.

Names like these used to strike terror in the hearts of humans. Some still do. It seems like every century has its own plague, and for humans and dogs in the twenty-first century, that plague is cancer.

Cancer is as rampant in dogs as it is in humans, rating number one out of the ten most common fatal diseases in purebred dogs. Half of all dogs who die over the age of ten die of cancer. Nearly half of all dogs who die from a natural disease die of cancer.

Described as a genetic disease, cancer becomes a greater risk as dogs age. Statistics show that one dog in five will develop cancer, the most common of which is skin cancer. As with humans, lighter-skinned dogs are greater targets for skin cancer, but the condition can strike any dog at any time. As previously discussed, you can avoid some cancers by neutering your dog before his first birthday.

Prevention

It's no news to us that a healthy lifestyle that includes wholesome food and plenty of exercise is crucial to avoiding cancer in dogs or humans. The same principles of a balanced diet with the necessary vitamins and minerals applies to both, and it is important to pay attention to cancer-prevention dietary guidelines.

Feed your APBT high-quality foods that meet his dietary needs and provide the extra elements thought to ward off cancer. Omega-3 fatty acids, for example, are a recommended dietary supplement, and they are abundant in fish. Add a little canned salmon to your dog's diet, or buy a commercial dog food that includes fish. Cruciferous vegetables (e.g., broccoli, cauliflower, brussels sprouts) help ward off gastrointestinal cancers. Keep in mind, though, that some foods that humans eat are not processed well in a dog's system. The last thing you want to do when trying to keep your APBT healthy is to make him sick. Be careful not to unintentionally deprive your APBT of the nutrients that carnivores need, and check with your vet before adding any dietary supplements.

Symptoms

Early detection of cancer can save, or at least extend, your dog's life, so be observant of your pet. Many of the early warning signs of cancer in humans are the same as for dogs, with a few more.

When you are petting or grooming your dog, feel around his entire body for bumps, lumps, sores, or anything out of the ordinary. Take note of how much water he drinks and how well he eats. (Increased or decreased thirst and/or appetite can be the first sign of illness.) Monitor his energy level and general mood. A dog who doesn't feel well may be lethargic and depressed. Many of these same signs are symptomatic of other health issues besides cancer, so don't expect the worst if you notice one or more of them in your APBT. The best thing to do in this situation is to bring him to the vet for a thorough evaluation.

Cancer Warning Signs

If you observe any of these symptoms in your APBT, have him checked out by the vet. Chances are it's nothing serious, but it is always better to be safe than sorry.

- Bad breath
- Bleeding or discharge from any body cavity
- Breathing difficulties
- Eating and/or swallowing difficulties
- Fatigue and general lethargy
- Lack of appetite
- Persistent stiffness or lameness
- Problems with elimination
- Recurrent sores or sores that won't heal
- Unusual lumps or bumps that grow
- Weight loss

Treatments

Cancer treatments vary with cancer types. A dog with bone cancer may undergo radiation, while a dog suffering from lymphoma will have a complex protocol of chemotherapy. The stage of the disease's development is also factored into the treatment plan. Some cancers are more aggressive than others and require more aggressive treatment.

Today pet health insurance policies are available to help defray veterinary costs. Insurance policies typically don't cover pre-existing conditions, so if you plan to obtain pet health insurance coverage, do it when your dog is still young. Not only do you want the best coverage at the best price, but if you prefer

Monitor your APBT's energy level and general mood, because a dog who doesn't feel well may be lethargic and depressed.

a specific veterinarian, you must see if she is a member of the plan's approved provider list, or choose an insurance plan that allows you to select your own veterinarian. Make sure the coverage includes cancer diagnosis and treatment.

Because cancer is a genetic disease, breeders should not breed dogs whose parents, grandparents, and siblings (even from different litters) develop cancer. This can be tricky, because cancer often waits until a dog's golden years to show up. By that time, unfortunately, the dog may have been bred one or more times.

We can't expect to wipe cancer out completely, but various preventive measures and treatment plans offer hope for generations of canines to come.

Congenital Heart Disease

APBTs should be checked for heart problems—congenital or otherwise—prior to breeding. Various types of heart disease are possible, and it makes sense for breeders to have their dogs screened.

Valvular Disease

The heart contains four valves: the mitral valve (left AV), tricuspid valve (right AV), aortic or left semilunar valve, and the pulmonic or right semilunar valve. The most common indication of valve trouble is a heart murmur, a particular sound made by the dysfunctional valves and heard with a stethoscope.

Valvular dysfunction is either congenital or acquired. Types of valvular disease include *endocarditis*, a bacterial infection that affects young to middle-aged, large-breed dogs with no history of heart disease; *congenital aortic stenosis*, a narrowing of the outflow channel between the left ventricle and the main artery of the body, the aorta; *congenital pulmonic valve stenosis*, which is a partial obstruction of normal blood flow to the lungs, usually due to a malformed pulmonary valve; and *canine dilated cardiomyopathy*, in which a flaccidity of the heart muscle prevents the heart from pumping properly and ultimately causes congestive heart failure.

Pericardial Disease

The pericardium is a protective sac surrounding the heart and major vessels. When diseased, it can cause a life-threatening restriction of the ventricles. Symptoms may include vomiting and labored breathing, or clinical signs may be absent. A stethoscope will detect muffled or displaced heart sounds that will alert the vet to heart trouble.

Screening for Heart Disease

APBTs should be checked for heart problems before they are bred, as various types of heart disease are possible in this breed.

Patent Ductus Arteriosis

Patent ductus arteriosis (PDA) is a birth defect that is the second most common congenital heart defect in dogs. It is an open vessel connecting the aorta with the pulmonary artery; this opening should close after a puppy is born. If it remains open, or *patent*, too much blood is passed into the lungs. Approximately 60 percent of afflicted dogs die within a year of diagnosis. Symptoms include coughing, lethargy, breathing difficulty, and exercise intolerance. If caught early, surgical closure of the duct should result in a normal life for the dog.

Gastrointestinal Disorders

Giant breeds like the Great Dane and barrel-chested breeds like the APBT are subject to special gastrointestinal problems less often seen in other breed types. It is a good idea to become familiar with these problems and decide what action to take if you suspect your dog has one.

Gastric Torsion (Bloat)

Gastric torsion, or *bloat* is a serious health concern for APBTs and other deep-chested breeds. Bloat occurs when the stomach, which has been distended from gas, water, or both, swells and twists. An otherwise healthy dog can die a painful death from gastric torsion in a matter of hours.

When torsion occurs, the esophagus closes off, limiting the dog's ability to relieve distention by vomiting or belching. The stomach becomes as taut as a drum, causing severe pain. The distended abdomen pushes against the lungs, making breathing difficult, and presses against the vena cava, the large transport vessel of blood from the abdominal area to the heart. When this blood flow is restricted, heart failure ultimately occurs. Immediate surgery is crucial to saving your dog's life.

Although some APBTs have a genetic predisposition to it, bloat may more often be the result of certain external factors. Some studies have found that bloat can be caused by the following:

Bloat Defined

Bloat occurs when the stomach swells and twists after becoming distended from gas, water, or both. This often fatal condition is a serious health concern for APBTs and other deep-chested breeds.

- Strenuous exercise after a large meal and/or large water intake. (A stomach heavy with food can be twisted out of place by strenuous activity. Also, gulping lots of water may result in the pet swallowing large amounts of air.)
- Mealtime agitation and stress. (May result in the dog swallowing large amounts of air.)
- Gender and age. (Males and dogs over two years of age seem to be more often afflicted.)
- Eating too fast. (May result in the pet swallowing large amounts of air.)
- Eating off the ground or floor. (Causes too much air intake during feeding. An elevated food dish will reduce this factor.)
- Eating only one meal per day. (If the dog is very hungry, he will gulp his food and swallow large amounts of air. An engorged stomach can twist out of position, starting a deadly chain of events.)

How will you know if your APBT is experiencing gastric torsion? The dramatic symptoms are very telling:

- Obvious abdominal pain and swelling
- Excessive drooling and panting
- Dazed, "shocky" look

- Repeated attempts to vomit
- Pale, cool-to-the-touch skin in and around the mouth

If you see any of these signs in your dog, seek immediate help, and don't panic. Call ahead so the vet can prepare for your arrival. They will first try to decompress the stomach with a stomach tube. Often this takes care of the situation, but if it doesn't, immediate surgery is required to correct the twisted stomach, remove unhealthy tissue, and anchor the stomach in place to avoid recurrences of bloat.

This stomach-anchoring procedure, called *gastropexy*, is sometimes performed as a preventive measure on dogs with a tendency toward bloat who have had bouts of distension or whose close relatives were victims of bloat. Gastropexy is a drastic measure that should be considered only if other preventive efforts have failed. Simple changes like increasing the frequency of your dog's meals, refraining from strenuous exercise right after meals, and not allowing him to drink large amounts of water right after exercising are much better ways to prevent this dangerous condition.

Giardiasis

Giardiasis is a gastrointestinal condition sometimes confused with worm infestation. Giardia are not worms; they're one-celled protozoa that mature in a dog's intestine. Diarrhea may be seen in afflicted dogs, but often no signs of illness are present at all. Giardiasis is not life threatening except in puppies and weakened adults. It produces severe, watery diarrhea. Diagnosis is through microscopic examination of a stool sample or through a blood test. Treatment is with an antibiotic that kills the giardia. Fluid replacement is also administered in cases of diarrhea.

Orthopedic Disorders

Orthopedic disorders affect the way in which a dog's skeletal system operates. If your APBT suffers from any problems in this area, he may have trouble walking and experience a great deal of discomfort.

Hip Dysplasia

Hip dysplasia is a painful, debilitating congenital disease that eventually can cause lameness and painful arthritis. A defect that creates a malformed hip joint, it is caused by a combination of genetic and environmental factors and is found in many dog breeds.

In a healthy hip, the thighbone (femur) joins the hip in the hip joint. In a dysplastic hip, the femur doesn't fit well into the too-shallow hip socket. The bone can then slide out of the socket, causing considerable pain.

Hip dysplasia almost always appears by the time the dog is 18 months old. Effects run the gamut from mild stiffness to severe crippling. No real cure is available, although surgery can ease the symptoms. In extreme cases, a complete hip replacement not only restores mobility but prevents recurrence, since the entire joint is replaced. A complete hip replacement provides the highest success rate but is very expensive. Prevention through genetic screening is the best way to go.

You, the owner, can do your part by being careful not to overfeed your puppy or adolescent APBT. The immature bone structure of puppies may not stand up to their body weight, especially when they are young and very active. Overexercising young dogs before their muscles and bones are fully developed may also contribute to hip problems later. To play it very safe, you can keep your APBT a little on the lean side until he's around two years old. By that time, his bones will be fully developed and capable of carrying the muscular load of an adult APBT.

Ear Disorders

In a healthy ABPT, ear care is usually low maintenance. A routine visual check when he's being groomed or loved is usually all it takes to make sure all is as it should be. The inside skin of the outer ear should be clean, pink, and smooth. If an ear problem exists, your dog will tell you by frequently shaking his head or pawing at his ear. Take a look—is there irritation and redness? Is there a discharge and/or an odor? If you answered "yes" to any of these questions, your APBT may be suffering from an ear infection.

There's a school of thought that cropped ears are less likely to become infected than uncropped ears. This is not true. Some breeds with very pendulous ears, like the Basset Hound, may be prone to ear infections because of the continually warm, moist environment inside the ear. The natural ear of the APBT is

Cropped Versus Uncropped Ears

Some people believe that cropped ears are less likely to become infected than uncropped ears, but this is not true. The natural ear of the APBT is fairly short and allows plenty of air circulation.

already fairly short, though, and it allows plenty of air circulation. Cropping doesn't make a difference.

Because the natural ear of the APBT allows plenty of air circulation, this breed is not particularly prone to ear infections.

Ear Mites

The most common ear disorder is ear mite infestation. These parasites usually affect the outer ear canal, although other parts of the ear can be affected, too. They cause itching and irritation, triggering the dog to shake his head and scratch his ears, worsening the irritation. Ear mites will leave dark brown droppings in the outer ear, coupled with a foul smell. Your vet will prescribe a treatment to flush out the ears and kill any eggs. An entire month of treatment is required to cure the infection. A relatively newer medication on the market requires only a single treatment.

Yeast Infections

Yeast organisms are rarely the main cause of ear infections, but they have no compunction about invading ears that are already moist and red with irritation, providing yeast with a prime breeding ground. Yeast inflammation is often a side effect of antibiotics, and it affects ears and/or toes. It is usually easy to identify: a thick, whitish discharge and a yeasty smell.

Yeast infections cause intense itching. The dog will scratch his ear, which will make the irritation worse. A common home remedy for yeast infection is a diluted vinegar wash, but vinegar can sting, making treatment unpleasant for your dog. It also won't take care of the primary cause of the infection. A visit to the vet will take care of both.

Aural Hematomas

This is a fairly common problem seen in all breeds, most often in retrievers. An aural hematoma is a swelling of the earflap. Blood vessels in the ear rupture, causing the space between the skin and the cartilage to fill with blood or serum. The cause of this is unclear (as with human nosebleeds), although often underlying things are going on (ear mites, porcupine quills, or allergies) that account for the excess pressure and inflammation.

Left untreated, the ear will become painful, and scarring will occur. Medical treatments do not always work, but you should try them before resorting to surgical correction. Your vet can prescribe medications to ease the pain and make your pet more comfortable.

Fly Strike

Fly strike occurs when flies target your APBT's ears for a bite-a-thon. Initially, they are attracted to the ear perhaps by earwax, a cut or wound, or the scent of an infection. The dog will scratch at the fly bites, worsening the irritation and causing bleeding that attracts more flies. The cycle seems unending and will make your dog miserable.

To prevent fly attacks, remove your APBT from the area and clean up his ears. Your vet may recommend products that you already have in the house. Outside, get rid of the flies by removing garbage or any other attraction.

Eye Disorders

A common quest among breeders, vets, and breed clubs is to reduce inherited eye disorders. When buying an APBT, one of the medical certifications you want is on the dog's genetic eye history. APBTs are not specifically prone to eye disorders, but terriers as a group have a predilection to some. A few are mentioned here.

Cataracts

Like our human eyes, dogs' eyes have a clear lens that helps focus about a third of their vision. Any cloudiness of that lens is called a *cataract*. Cataracts may be very slight and not interfere with vision; may involve part of the lens, blurring vision; or cloud the entire lens, causing loss of all functional vision.

What is not a cataract? All geriatric dogs experience a hardening of the lens called nuclear sclerosis. It makes the lens look grayish and may fool the owner into thinking it is a cataract. Nuclear sclerosis is a normal byproduct of aging and does not usually interfere with the dog's vision. This is not to say that senior dogs do not develop cataracts; they do, often after the age of eight. Cataracts may develop quickly over weeks and months, or they may grow slowly over the years in one or both eyes. It is usually an inherited trait, so affected dogs should not be used for breeding. Cataracts can also develop in diabetic dogs or orphaned puppies on a milk-replacement diet. Environmental factors, such as extreme heat, radiation, or exposure to chemicals, can contribute to cataract formation. So can eye diseases like persistent papillary membrane (PPM) and progressive retinal atrophy (PRA).

Once a cataract has developed, it is not possible to make the lens clear again. This used to mean blindness, but now the same artificial lens replacement practiced on humans is available for dogs with cataracts. A small incision is made in the eye, and a hole is made in the small sac that holds the lens. A special probe ultrasonically emulsifies and removes the affected lens, and an artificial replacement called an *intraocular lens*, or *IOL*, is placed in the sac. The incision is closed with incredibly small sutures that are finer than a strand of hair. The entire surgery is performed with an operating microscope under high magnification.

Lens replacement surgery provides a solution to those dogs suffering from cataracts. Although the surgery does not guarantee perfect vision, it can help.

Lens replacement surgery does not guarantee perfect vision. The artificial lens (IOL) should match the original lens as closely as possible, but only so many IOLs are available for dogs. Dogs' eyes tend to have more inflammation after surgery than human eyes, causing more scarring, and scarring blurs vision. Still, the cornea is responsible for two-thirds of vision focusing, so if the lens isn't perfect or can't be replaced, the dog will still have functional vision.

Lens Luxation

Primary lens luxation is a congenital eye disease that occurs when the lens moves from its normal position behind the cornea. Secondary lens luxation occurs when an injury dislodges the lens.

Lens luxation occurs when fibers holding the lens in place break, allowing the lens to shift forward or backward, thus interfering with healthy eye functions. This disruption can lead to glaucoma or even blindness, depending on where the untethered lens ultimately rests. The breeder's problem is that symptoms don't appear until the dog is three years old, by which time he may have been bred.

The first signs of lens luxation may be behavioral changes due to vision changes (bumping into things, trouble catching balls). Pain may cause the dog to paw at the eye. Treatment depends on how soon the condition is discovered. In all cases, surgery is required, either to remove the entire lens and replace it with an artificial lens, or to remove some of the eye fluid that is causing glaucoma. If luxation damages the optic nerve and blindness results, no effective treatment is possible. The damaged eye may be painful, in which case the eye will be surgically removed or replaced with a prosthesis.

Untreated, lens luxation can lead to glaucoma or corneal edema.

Persistent Pupillary Membranes (PPM)

PPMs are vestiges of blood vessels that fed the developing eye of a dog fetus. They usually disappear by four or five months of age, but sometimes they persist. PPM may interfere with vision, but many dogs with PPM have no problems at all. Extreme cases, though, can lead to partial or total vision loss. Although the vet can detect them with an ophthalmic scope during routine checkups, no real treatment exists unless cataracts result.

Progressive Retinal Atrophy (PRA)

This inherited disorder refers to the degeneration of vision cells in the retina, which causes blindness. Early symptoms include loss of night vision, which will make the dog reluctant to go outside at night or into darkened areas inside. Loss of day vision follows, and sometimes cataracts occur. No treatment for PRA is available, which is why annual examinations by a veterinary ophthalmologist (your regular vet will not have the right equipment) for PRA are important for breeding stock.

HOW TO ADMINISTER MEDICATION

At some point in your APBT's life, you will probably need to give him medication. Dogs are not the most cooperative patients, so it helps to know how to administer medications with a minimum of stress for both of you.

Applying Eye Drops

- Gently tilt the dog's head back so that he is looking upward.
- Use your thumb and index finger to gently hold open his eyelids.
- Drop the prescribed number of drops directly onto the eye.
- Keep the dog's head tilted upward for about ten seconds so that the drops don't roll out prematurely.

Applying Eye Ointment

- Gently tilt the dog's head back so that he is looking upward.
- Gently pull the lower eyelid down and squeeze a thin line of ointment inside the narrow well between the eyeball and the lid.
- Close the eye and very lightly massage the closed lids to distribute the ointment over the eye.

Applying Ear Drops

- Gently pull the tip of the dog's ear upward across his head toward his other ear so that you can easily see the ear canal.
- Squeeze the prescribed number of drops into the ear canal.
- Continue holding the dog's head to prevent him from shaking it and sending the medication drops flying. Gently massage the area just below the ear for a few seconds to help the medicine travel into the inner ear.

EMERGENCY CARE

Humans are lucky. All we have to do is dial for help and an ambulance will speed to our aid. But what happens if your APBT has an accident or is otherwise in need of immediate medical attention? No ambulance is going to come racing to

Medical Emergencies

The following should be considered medical emergencies requiring immediate care:
- heatstroke
- hypothermia
- frostbite
- poisoning

help a dog, much less an APBT. You might likewise find it difficult to come upon willing helpers who aren't afraid of your APBT, especially if he has been in a fight. Veterinary house calls are rare, and in a true emergency, impractical. It is best to know how to evaluate an emergency yourself and safely transport your APBT to the hospital.

Purchase a canine emergency first-aid manual and read through it a few times. Don't wait until the accident or emergency happens to read up on what to do. Keep the phone number and driving directions to the nearest after-hours clinic handy. Emergencies don't wait until Monday morning, and you don't want to waste precious time trying to find a vet on a Sunday night.

Heatstroke

Dogs do not sweat like humans sweat, but they do have their own system of cooling themselves down. They perspire a little through their paws, but their primary cooling method is panting. Rapid panting exchanges hot air for cool air. The problem is that on sweltering days there just isn't much cool air. You may have noticed that, after exercise, your APBT's tongue appears larger than usual. That's because it is. The tongue swells to increase the surface area and allow more air to pass over it. The blood vessels in the tongue then distribute the cooled blood

First-Aid Kit

Keep these items on hand for emergencies. Check periodically to see if anything needs to be replaced or if medications have spilled or dried up.

- Activated charcoal tablets
- Adhesive tape
- Antibacterial ointment
- Aspirin (not ibuprofen)
- Cotton balls
- Antidiarrhea medicine, such as Imodium or Pepto-Bismol
- Dosing syringe
- Gauze bandages and pads

- Hydrogen peroxide (3 percent)
- Latex gloves
- Petroleum jelly
- Rectal thermometer
- Rubbing alcohol
- Scissors
- Towel
- Tweezers

Never leave your APBT alone in a warm car, even for a few minutes, as he could suffer from heatstroke.

through the body. Unfortunately, these cooling systems are not as efficient as those of the human body, thus leaving dogs more susceptible to heatstroke.

You should suspect heatstroke if your APBT is exposed to very hot temperatures and exhibits the following symptoms:

- Rapid mouth breathing
- Increased heart/pulse rate
- Reddened gums
- Vomiting
- Moisture accumulating on feet
- Thickened saliva
- A dazed expression

Heatstroke requires immediate action to save the dog's life. For mild cases, bring the dog to a cooler environment and give him cold water to drink. If he seems unsteady on his feet or has a high temperature, put him in a cool bath or shower. (If the water is too cold, peripheral blood vessel constriction can occur, slowing the cooling process.) See a vet immediately.

Hypothermia

For breeds like the Eskimo Dog, Siberian Husky, and the Malamute, their fur coats allow them to remain comfortable outside in cold temperatures. The APBT's short coat, on the other hand, does little to insulate him for very long in extremely cold temperatures without shelter. Add precipitation to the scenario, and you are putting your dog in danger of hypothermia.

If your APBT is shivering uncontrollably, has a low (below 100°F [37.8°C]) body temperature, and seems fatigued, wrap him in a blanket, jacket, towel, or whatever is immediately available. Take him to a warm room and rub his fur dry with a towel. You can use a blow dryer as long as it is set to warm, not hot. Gradually raise his body temperature to 100°F (37.8°C) by applying warm water bottles or warm packs to his body, or have him recline on a carefully monitored electric blanket on a low setting. If your dog's temperature doesn't reach 100°F (37.8°C), or if he is unconscious, rush him to the vet immediately.

Frostbite

Sometimes a companion to hypothermia, frostbite can affect dogs on their extremities—toes, ears, scrotum, or tail tip—just as it affects humans. As the blood supply to the affected area diminishes, the skin becomes pale. It turns red, swells, and becomes itchy and painful when blood circulation returns during treatment.

When treating frostbite, thaw out affected areas by applying towels soaked in tepid water to the area for about 15 to 20 minutes. Avoid rubbing or squeezing, which can aggravate the injury. If the area remains red and swollen, seek immediate help. Your vet will prescribe antibiotics to kill infection, and if needed, pain relievers. Quick treatment is the key to preventing amputation or death from frostbite injury.

If Your APBT Becomes Lost

If your APBT becomes lost, follow the steps listed below to increase the chances that you will be reunited with your canine companion.

- Walk the neighborhood, talk to everyone, and leave your phone number in case someone spots your dog.
- Talk to the mail carrier, paper deliverer, or anyone you encounter. Give them a description of the dog and your phone number.
- Use a dog whistle while you search. The high-pitched sound can carry up to a mile or more.
- Put some strong-scented clothing outside your home on the lawn or driveway. Sweaty gym socks may just be the beacon that guides your dog home!
- Call veterinarians' offices to see if anyone has brought in an unfamiliar dog. Also, check with all area shelters and animal control agencies.
- Post flyers everywhere you can within a mile of where your dog was lost. Omit your name and address so that scam artists won't take advantage of it. Offer a reward, but don't specify the amount. Withhold descriptions of a few unique identifying marks or characteristics of your APBT. You will use these for further identification if someone says they have your pet. Unfortunately, some people will say they have your pet but are just looking for upfront money. They may also try to pass off another dog as yours.
- If your APBT is microchipped, notify the company with whom the dog is registered, and hope that someone will find him and have him scanned for identification. If he is tattooed, there is a chance it might be seen. However, tattoos can be difficult to read, and dog thieves have been known to cut off a tattooed ear. If you do choose to tattoo your dog for identification purposes, do it on the inner thigh. Hopefully the finder will spot it and call the hotline.

Poison

The world is filled with poisons, both chemical and natural. No matter how conscientious we are about safeguarding our pets, they are sometimes exposed to these dangers. Here is an overview of some of the most common poisons lurking in your surroundings:

In the House

- **Prescription and nonprescription medications, dietary supplements, cosmetics, and perfumes:** Keep them off countertops and vanities where resourceful APBTs can get to them.

- **Household cleaners:** Keep them out of sight, out of mind, out of reach.
- **Toilet bowl continuous sanitizers:** Whether blue or clear, they are toxic if your APBT decides to drink from the toilet. Keep the toilet lid down or refrain from use.
- **Houseplants:** Many, such as poinsettias and chrysanthemums, are poisonous. Find out if your decorative plants are toxic, and if so, put them out of your APBT's reach.
- **Foods commonly found in kitchens, like chocolate, onions, and macadamia nuts:** Some foods we enjoy are pure poison to dogs. Check before sharing.

In the Yard

- **Pesticides, herbicides, and insecticides such as slug bait, Japanese beetle traps, rodent traps and killers, weed killers:** Chances are, if you have an APBT, you're too busy

Poisonous Plants

Rid your yard of these dangerous plants and keep your ABPT safe.

• American Blue Flag	• Fern	• Mullein
• Bachelor's Button	• Foxglove	• Narcissus
• Barberry	• Hellebore	• Peony
• Bog Iris	• Herb of Grace	• Persian Ivy
• Boxwood	• Holly	• Rhododendron
• Buttercup	• Horse Chestnut	• Rhubarb
• Cherry Pits	• Iris Bulbs	• Shallon
• Chinese Arbor	• Japanese Yew	• Siberian Iris
• Chokecherry	• Jerusalem Cherry	• Solomon's Seal
• Climbing Lily	• Jimson Weed	• Star of Bethlehem
• Crown of Thorns	• Lily of the Valley	• Water Lily
• Elderberry berries	• Marigold	• Wisteria
• Elephant Ear	• Milkwort	• Wood Spurge
• English Ivy	• Mistletoe Berries	• Yew
• False Acacia	• Monkshood	

Inspect your yard for common outdoor foliage, because some plants can cause skin irritation.

keeping him exercised to maintain a pristine flower garden anyway. Reconcile yourself to having a less-than-perfect lawn if you have a pet.

- **Common outdoor plants:** Some outdoor plants can cause skin irritation, while others can kill your dog. Take note of the types of plants growing in your yard, and remove hazards to your APBT's health.
- **Some snakes, some spiders, scorpions, and bees:** Venomous bites from snakes, scorpions, and spiders can make your dog very sick and possibly kill him. And although bees are not venomous, an allergic reaction to their stings can trigger allergic anaphylaxis, a potentially life-threatening systemic reaction.

In the Garage

- **Antifreeze:** The sweet taste of antifreeze attracts pets … and kills them.
- **Paint and paint thinners:** Both are poisonous if swallowed.
- **Sharp gardening or landscaping implements:**

193

Blades can cause serious injury.
- **Exposed insulation:** The contents of building insulation (glass, sand, rock wool, fiberglass, cellulose) can sicken or kill a dog if consumed.
- **Car cleaning products:** Their chemical contents are potentially deadly.
- **Gasoline:** If ingested, it can kill your dog or at least make him very sick. If gasoline vapors are inhaled continually, benzene poisoning can cause cancer and/or serious illness.

If Your APBT Is Injured

Alternative approaches to canine health are growing in popularity. These approaches include:
- acupuncture
- chiropractic
- homeopathy
- herbal therapy

Preparation will help you keep a cool head and be of the most help to your injured APBT. Here are some common-sense rules to remember when your pet is hurt:

1. Stay calm and speak to the dog in a reassuring voice.
2. Always approach an injured animal slowly and cautiously, even if it is your lifelong friend.
3. Gently muzzle the dog to prevent fear biting. Use a necktie or scarf as a makeshift muzzle, and learn how to apply it.
4. Use a tabletop or sturdy piece of wood as a makeshift stretcher to carry the dog.
5. Apply pressure to stop any bleeding.
6. Call the vet, and drive safely to the animal hospital.

ALTERNATIVE HEALTH CARE THERAPIES

Over the last few decades, many pet owners have become interested in alternative approaches to animal health care. *Alternative* or *holistic* medicine purports that wellness and illness result from combined emotional and physical factors. Ancient disciplines like acupuncture, reiki, and herbal therapy are utilized in holistic health care, as well as more mainstream treatments like chiropractic and massage therapy.

Holistic medicine advocates the use of natural remedies, usually ingredients found in plants. It has a presence in modern veterinary care, although holistic vets are not always easy to find. This may change as more veterinarians branch out into alternative treatments. As with human health care, it's a good idea to find a balance between alternative remedies and scientific medicine, taking advantage of all available resources to ensure a long, healthy life for your APBT.

The following are some brief descriptions of just a few of the many alternative approaches to canine health care that are available.

Acupuncture

Literally translated as "needle piercing," acupuncture is the practice of inserting very fine needles into the skin to stimulate specific anatomic points in the body for healing purposes. Practiced for centuries by the Chinese, the purpose of acupuncture is to restore good health by regulating the life force, known as *qi*. Over the past 40 years, it has become a well-known, fairly available form of treatment in developing and underdeveloped countries. In the West, acupuncture is regarded as a complement to conventional medicine. Holistic veterinarians practice this painless procedure as a companion treatment for a variety of health issues.

Chiropractic

The word "chiropractic" comes from the Greek for "hand practice." The philosophy behind this treatment is based on the relationship of the spinal column to the nervous and circulatory systems, as well as to biomechanics and movement. Chiropractors manipulate the vertebrae to alter disease progression and relieve many joint, nerve, and muscle problems.

Homeopathy

Based on the principle that "like cures like," homeopathy formulates remedies for the same symptoms caused by the primary remedy ingredient alone. For example, ipecac syrup is used to induce vomiting. But in a homeopathic version, ipecac can help eliminate vomiting. Homeopathic medicines are highly diluted forms of the original substance that are thought to stimulate the patient's life force to begin the healing process. Holistic veterinarians are becoming more prevalent, and veterinary homeopathy can be a helpful companion to conventional medical treatment.

Herbal Therapy

Herbs have been used for their curative properties since the dawn of humankind, and they are still the purest, simplest way to use medicine as nature intended. The restorative effects of herbs are safe for dogs as well as humans. Before giving any herbal treatment, though, always consult your veterinarian. Drug interactions, allergic reactions, and herbal product quality are important considerations to be explored with your veterinarian before embarking on a program of herbal therapy.

TWILIGHT TIME

It's bound to happen—that adorable APBT puppy grows up and gets old. A healthy APBT could live with you for 12 to 15 years, but at some point, he will become a grizzled senior citizen. APBTs may be perennial puppies at heart, but eventually your dog will sleep a little more and play a little less vigorously and for less duration. His teeth and gums may need extra care, and his stomach may become sensitive and require a food formulated especially for older dogs. His hearing or sight may deteriorate. In fact, elderly dogs experience many of the same physical changes as humans do when they age—they just handle them better than we do. You can't fight Mother Nature, but you can make it easier to deal with her. Keep up with your regular vet visits, and you'll see how easily managed most aging issues are.

Even the happiest and healthiest of APBTs reach the end of their days with us. Modern medicine and quality health care have extended the life spans of our pets, but these advances have also opened them up to additional diseases. Today, relatively few dogs pass away in their sleep from old age. Chances are you will one day be faced with the issue of euthanasia.

The hardest part is not deciding whether to put an end to your dog's suffering; it's knowing when the time is right. Your vet will help you with this decision, and so will your APBT. You both established your own brand of communication with each other throughout his life; he won't fail you now. As much as he wants to please you by continuing to live, the physical effort of hanging on may be too difficult for him. In typical APBT manner, he may be in more pain than he's revealing. Because of

Cognitive Dysfunction Syndrome—Dog "Senility"

Cognitive Dysfunction Syndrome (CDS) is the gradual deterioration of cognitive abilities, indicated by behavioral changes. If a dog's typical behavior changes and no specific physical malady is the cause, suspect CDS. More than half of dogs over the age of eight years of age suffer from some form of CDS. Symptoms include:

- **Frequent elimination in the house.** Your dog doesn't communicate that he needs to go outside to eliminate.
- **Change in sleep patterns.** Your dog sleeps more than normal during the day and sleeps less during the night
- **Confusion.** Your dog goes outside and just stands there, has a dazed look in his eyes, doesn't come when called, walks around listlessly, and doesn't recognize friends.
- **Failure to respond to social stimuli.** Your dog doesn't tolerate much petting, doesn't respond to you when you return home, and doesn't come to people as much, whether called or not.

this, you will need to pick up on the signals given by dogs near death. They may pant heavily, refuse food and water, or hide themselves in a protected or secluded area.

After all that you and your good dog have been through together, nothing is harder than saying goodbye. When the time comes, try to handle it like an APBT: Hang tough until the end, remembering that the greatest love is knowing when to let go.

Good health is a gift. We need to show our appreciation for this gift by taking care of ourselves and the pets who rely on us for everything. With good food, plenty of exercise, a lot of love, and regular veterinary care, our APBTs will continue to enrich our lives for many happy years.

"The greatness of a nation and its moral progress can be judged by the way its animals are treated."
—Gandhi

THE UNITED KENNEL CLUB BREED STANDARD

Revised October 21, 2004

History Sometime during the nineteenth century, dog fanciers in England, Ireland, and Scotland began to experiment with crosses between Bulldogs and Terriers, looking for a dog that combined the gameness of the terrier with the strength and athleticism of the Bulldog. The result was a dog that embodied all of the virtues attributed to great warriors: strength, indomitable courage, and gentleness with loved ones. Immigrants brought these bull and terrier crosses to the United States. The American Pit Bull Terrier's many talents did not go unnoticed by farmers and ranchers who used their APBTs for protection, as catch dogs for semi-wild cattle and hogs, to hunt, to drive livestock, and as family companions. Today, the American Pit Bull Terrier continues to demonstrate its versatility, competing successfully in Obedience, Tracking, Agility, Protection, and Weight Pulls, as well as Conformation.

The United Kennel Club was the first registry to recognize the American Pit Bull Terrier. U.K.C. founder C. Z. Bennett assigned U.K.C. registration number 1 to his own APBT, Bennett's Ring in 1898.

General Appearance The American Pit Bull Terrier is a medium-sized, solidly built, short-coated dog with smooth, well-defined musculature. This breed is both powerful and athletic. The body is just slightly longer than tall, but bitches may be somewhat longer in body than dogs. The length of the front leg (measured from point of elbow to the ground) is approximately equal to one-half of the dog's height at the withers. The head is of medium length, with a broad, flat skull, and a wide, deep muzzle. Ears are small to medium in size, high set, and may be natural or cropped. The relatively short tail is set low, thick at the base and tapers to a point. The American Pit Bull Terrier comes in all colors and color patterns. This breed combines strength and athleticism with grace and agility and should never appear bulky or muscle-bound or fine-boned and rangy.

Characteristics The essential characteristics of the American Pit Bull Terrier are strength, confidence, and zest for life. This breed is eager to please and brimming over with enthusiasm. APBTs make excellent family companions and have always been noted for their love of children. Because most APBTs exhibit some level of dog aggression and because of its powerful physique, the APBT requires an owner who will carefully socialize and obedience train the dog. The breed's natural agility makes it one of the most capable canine climbers so good fencing is a must for this breed. The APBT is not the best choice for a guard dog since they are extremely friendly, even with strangers. Aggressive behavior toward humans is uncharacteristic of the breed and highly undesirable. This breed does very well in performance events because of its high level of intelligence and its willingness to work.

The American Pit Bull Terrier has always been capable of doing a wide variety of jobs so exaggerations or faults should be penalized in proportion to how much they interfere with the dog's versatility.

Head The APBT head is unique and a key element of breed type. It is large and broad, giving the impression of great power, but it is not disproportionate to the size of the body. Viewed from the front, the head is shaped like a broad, blunt wedge. When viewed from the side, the skull and muzzle are parallel to one another and joined by a well defined, moderately deep stop. Supraorbital arches over the eyes are well defined but not pronounced. The head is well chiseled, blending strength, elegance, and character.

SKULL - The skull is large, flat or slightly rounded, deep, and broad between the ears. Viewed from the top, the skull tapers just slightly toward the stop. There is a deep median furrow that diminishes in depth from the stop to the occiput. Cheek muscles are prominent but free of wrinkles. When the dog is concentrating, wrinkles form on the forehead, which give the APBT his unique expression.

MUZZLE - The muzzle is broad and deep with a very slight taper from the stop to the nose, and a slight falling away under the eyes. The length of muzzle is shorter than the length of skull, with a ratio of approximately 2:3. The topline of the muzzle is straight. The lower jaw is well developed, wide and deep. Lips are clean and tight.
Faults: Snipey muzzle; flews; weak lower jaw.
TEETH - The American Pit Bull Terrier has a complete set of evenly spaced, white teeth meeting in a scissors bite.
Fault: Level bite.
Serious Faults: Undershot, or overshot bite; wry mouth; missing teeth (this does not apply to teeth that have been lost or removed by a veterinarian).
NOSE - The nose is large with wide, open nostrils. The nose may be any color.
EYES - Eyes are medium size, round to almond-shaped, and set well apart and low on the skull. All colors are equally acceptable except blue, which is a serious fault. Haw should not be visible.
Serious Faults: Bulging eyes; both eyes not matched in color; blue eyes.
EARS - Ears are high set and may be natural or cropped without preference. If natural, semi-prick or rose are preferred. Prick or flat, wide ears are not desired.

Neck The neck is of moderate length and muscular. There is a slight arch at the crest. The neck widens gradually from where it joins the skull to where it blends into well laid-back shoulders. The skin on the neck is tight and without dewlap.
Faults: Neck too short and thick; thin or weak neck; ewe neck; dewlap.

Forequarters The shoulder blades are long, wide, muscular, and well laid back. The upper arm is roughly equal in length to the shoulder blade and joins it at an apparent right angle.
The forelegs are strong and muscular. The elbows are set close to the body. Viewed from the front, the forelegs are set moderately wide apart and perpendicular to the ground. The pasterns are short, powerful, straight, and flexible. When viewed in profile, the pasterns are nearly erect.
Faults: Upright or loaded shoulders; elbows turned outward or tied-in; down at the pasterns; front legs bowed; wrists knuckled over; toeing in or out.

Body The chest is deep, well filled in, and moderately wide with ample room for heart and lungs, but the chest should never be wider than it is deep. The forechest does not extend much beyond the point of shoulder. The ribs extend well back and are well sprung from the spine, then flattening to form a deep body extending to the elbows. The back is strong and firm. The topline inclines very slightly downward from the withers to a broad, muscular, level back. The loin is short, muscular and slightly arched to the top of the croup, but narrower than the rib cage and with a moderate tuck-up. The croup is slightly sloping downward.

Hindquarters The hindquarters are strong, muscular, and moderately broad. The rump is well filled in on each side of the tail and deep from the pelvis to the crotch. The bone, angulation, and musculature of the hindquarters are in balance with the forequarters. The thighs are well developed with thick, easily discerned muscles. Viewed from the side, the hock joint is well bent and the rear pasterns are well let down and perpendicular to the ground. Viewed from the rear, the rear pasterns are straight and parallel to one another.
Faults: Narrow hindquarters; hindquarters shallow from pelvis to crotch; lack of muscle; straight or over angulated stifle joint; cow hocks; sickle hocks; bowed legs.

Feet The feet are round, proportionate to the size of the dog, well arched, and tight. Pads are hard, tough, and well cushioned. Dewclaws may be removed.
Fault: Splayed feet.

Tail The tail is set on as a natural extension of the topline, and tapers to a point. When the dog is

relaxed, the tail is carried low and extends approximately to the hock. When the dog is moving, the tail is carried level with the backline. When the dog is excited, the tail may be carried in a raised, upright position (challenge tail), but never curled over the back (gay tail).
Fault: Long tail (tail tip passes beyond point of hock).
Serious faults: Gay tail (not to be confused with challenge tail); kinked tail.
Disqualification: Bobbed tail.

Coat The coat is glossy and smooth, close, and moderately stiff to the touch.
Faults: Curly, wavy, or sparse coat.
Disqualification: Long coat.

Color Any color, color pattern, or combination of colors is acceptable, except for merle.
Disqualification: Merle

Height and Weight

The American Pit Bull Terrier must be both powerful and agile so actual weight and height are less important than the correct proportion of weight to height. Desirable weight for a mature male in good condition is between 35 and 60 pounds. Desirable weight for a mature female in good condition is between 30 and 50 pounds. Dogs over these weights are not to be penalized unless they are disproportionately massive or rangy.

Gait The American Pit Bull Terrier moves with a jaunty, confident attitude, conveying the impression that he expects any minute to see something new and exciting. When trotting, the gait is effortless, smooth, powerful, and well coordinated, showing good reach in front and drive behind. When moving, the backline remains level with only a slight flexing to indicate suppleness. Viewed from any position, legs turn neither in nor out, nor do feet cross or interfere with each other. As speed increases, feet tend to converge toward center line of balance.
Faults: Legs not moving on the same plane; legs over reaching; legs crossing over in front or rear; rear legs moving too close or touching; rolling; pacing; paddling; sidewinding; hackney action; pounding.

Disqualifications Unilateral or bilateral cryptorchid. Viciousness or extreme shyness. Unilateral or bilateral deafness. Bobbed tail. Albinism. Merle.

Note: Although some level of dog aggression is characteristic of this breed, handlers will be expected to comply with U.K.C. policy regarding dog temperament at U.K.C. events.

ASSOCIATIONS AND ORGANIZATIONS

Breed Clubs

American Dog Breeders Association (ADBA)
P.O. Box 1771
S.L.C., UT 84110
Telephone: (801) 936-7513
Fax: (801) 936-4229
www.adba.cc

National American Pit Bull Terrier Association (NAPBTA)
Secretary: Shana Bobbitt
E-mail: starfroggie@gmail.com
www.napbta.com

United Kennel Club (UKC)
100 E. Kilgore Road
Kalamazoo, MI 49002-5584
Telephone: (269) 343-9020
Fax: (269) 343-7037
E-mail: pbickell@ukcdogs.com
www.ukcdogs.com

Rescue Organizations and Animal Welfare Groups

American Humane Association (AHA)
63 Inverness Drive East
Englewood, CO 80112
Telephone: (303) 792-9900
Fax: 792-5333
www.americanhumane.org

American Society for the Prevention of Cruelty to Animals (ASPCA)
424 E. 92nd Street
New York, NY 10128-6804
Telephone: (212) 876-7700
www.aspca.org

Pit Bull Rescue Central (PBRC)
www.pbrc.net

Royal Society for the Prevention of Cruelty to Animals (RSPCA)
Telephone: 0870 3335 999
Fax: 0870 7530 284
www.rspca.org.uk

The Humane Society of the United States (HSUS)
2100 L Street, NW
Washington DC 20037
Telephone: (202) 452-1100
www.hsus.org

Sports

Canine Freestyle Federation, Inc.
Membership Secretary: Brandy Clymire
E-mail: CFFmemberinfo@aol.com
www.canine-freestyle.org

International Agility Link (IAL)
Global Administrator: Steve Drinkwater
E-mail: yunde@powerup.au
www.agilityclick.com/~ial

North American Flyball Association (NAFA)
1400 West Devon Avenue #512
Chicago, IL 60660
Telephone: (800) 318-6312
Fax: (800) 318-6318
www.flyball.org

Veterinary Resources

Academy of Veterinary Homeopathy (AVH)
P.O. Box 9280
Wilmington, DE 19809
Telephone: (866) 652-1590
Fax: (866) 652-1590
E-mail: office@TheAVH.org
www.theavh.org

American Academy of Veterinary Acupuncture (AAVA)
100 Roscommon Drive, Suite 320
Middletown, CT 06457
Telephone: (860) 635-6300
Fax: (860) 635-6400
E-mail: office@aava.org
www.aava.org

American Animal Hospital Association (AAHA)
P.O. Box 150899
Denver, CO 80215-0899
Telephone: (303) 986-2800
Fax: (303) 986-1700
E-mail: info@aahanet.org
www.aahanet.org/index.cfm

American Holistic Veterinary Medical Association (AHVMA)
2218 Old Emmorton Road
Bel Air, MD 21015
Telephone: (410) 569-0795
Fax: (410) 569-2346
E-mail: office@ahvma.org
www.ahvma.org

American Veterinary Medical Association (AVMA)
1931 North Meacham Road – Suite 100
Schaumburg, IL 60173
Telephone: (847) 925-8070
Fax: (847) 925-1329
E-mail: avmainfo@avma.org
www.avma.org

British Veterinary Association (BVA)
7 Mansfield Street
London
W1G 9NQ
Telephone: 020 7636 6541
Fax: 020 7436 2970
E-mail: bvahq@bva.co.uk
www.bva.co.uk

Miscellaneous

Association of Pet Dog Trainers (APDT)
150 Executive Center Drive Box 35
Greenville, SC 29615
Telephone: (800) PET-DOGS
Fax: (864) 331-0767
E-mail: information@apdt.com
www.apdt.com

Delta Society
875 124th Ave NE, Suite 101
Bellevue, WA 98005
Telephone: (425) 226-7357
Fax: (425) 235-1076
E-mail: info@deltasociety.org
www.deltasociety.org

Therapy Dogs International (TDI)
88 Bartley Road
Flanders, NJ 07836
Telephone: (973) 252-9800
Fax: (973) 252-7171
E-mail: tdi@gti.net
www.tdi-dog.org

PUBLICATIONS

BOOKS

Lane, Dick, and Neil Ewart. A-Z of Dog Diseases & Health Problems. New York: Howell Books, 1997.

Rubenstein, Eliza, and Shari Kalina. *The Adoption Option: Choosing and Raising the Shelter Dog for You.* New York: Howell Books, 1996.

Serpell, James. *The Domestic Dog: Its Evolution, Behaviour and Interactions with People.* Cambridge: Cambridge University Press, 1995.

MAGAZINES

Dog & Kennel
Pet Publishing, Inc.
7-L Dundas Circle
Greensboro, NC 27407
Telephone: (336) 292-4272
Fax: (336) 292-4272
E-mail: info@petpublishing.com
www.dogandkennel.com

Dog Fancy
Subscription Department
P.O. Box 53264
Boulder, CO 80322-3264
Telephone: (800) 365-4421
E-mail: barkback@dogfancy.com
www.dogfancy.com

Dogs Monthly
Ascot House
High Street, Ascot,
Berkshire SL5 7JG
United Kingdom
Telephone: 0870 730 8433
Fax: 0870 730 8431
E-mail: admin@rtc-associates.freeserve.co.uk
www.corsini.co.uk/dogsmonthly

WEBSITES

Dog-Play
www.dog-play.com/ethics.html
A cornucopia of information and pertinent links on responsible dog breeding.

The Dog Speaks
www.thedogspeaks.com
Canine Behaviorist Deb Duncan's site, filled with useful advice on canine etiquette, behavior problems, communication, and relevant links.

Petfinder
www.petfinder.org
Search shelters and rescue groups for adoptable pets.

DEDICATION

For my mother, Phyllis Polansky

ACKNOWLEDGEMENTS

Sincere appreciation goes out to Ted Kedzierski and his APBT, Hurricane; editor extraordinaire Stephanie Fornino; and my husband, Kevin, for his ongoing love and support.

ABOUT THE AUTHOR

Cynthia P. Gallagher lives in Annapolis, Maryland with her husband and two Boxers. Her dog writing credits include ASPCA Animal Watch, Dog & Kennel, and Animal Fair magazines. She is also the author of two novels under the name Cynthia Polansky. Visit her website at www.cynthiapolansky.com.

PHOTO CREDITS

Photo on page 26 courtesy of Todd Adamson
Photo on page 50 courtesy of Mary Bloom
Photos on pages 11, 84, and 100 courtesy of Robert Pearcy
All other photos courtesy of Isabelle Francais and T.F.H. archives